Disability Politics

Understanding our past, changing our future

Jane Campbell and Mike Oliver

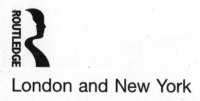

London and New York

First published 1996
by Routledge
11 New Fetter Lane, London EC4P 4EE

Simultaneously published in the USA and Canada
by Routledge
29 West 35th Street, New York, NY 10001

Routledge is an International Thomson Publishing company

Typeset in Palatino by Routledge
Printed and bound in Great Britain by
TJ Press (Padstow) Ltd, Padstow, Cornwall

British Library Cataloguing in Publication Data
A catalogue record for this book is available from the British Library

Library of Congress Cataloging in Publication Data
A catalogue record for this book has been requested

ISBN 0–415–07998–5 (hbk)
ISBN 0–415–07999–3 (pbk)

The last fifteen years have seen momentous changes in the profile of disabled people throughout Britain. Much of this is due to the rise of a powerful and vibrant social movement of disabled people. They have tackled both matters relating to their everyday lives and wider political issues. They have developed and promoted the idea of independent living and have forced major legislative changes to take place.

This book is written by disabled people and uses their own voices to describe those changes. It clearly traces the emergence and survival of the disability movement and provides an honest evaluation of its successes and failures. It then goes on to consider possible future directions for disabled people in twenty-first century Britain.

This book will help disabled people to understand their past and change their future. It is a significant contribution to history, social theory and policy, and political studies.

Jane Campbell has specialised in the areas of disability rights and independent living and was a recent Chair of the British Council of Disabled People. During her term in office she has seen the organisation through some of its most pioneering work in the field of independent living, civil rights, peer counselling and equal opportunities. She is currently running a training and project management consultancy in disability rights and independent living.

Mike Oliver is a disabled academic and political activist. He served on the management committees of SKILL and SIA when they were formed and he was a founding council member of the BCODP, in which he continues to be involved through their research sub-group. He is also a member of DAN. He is to date the only Professor of Disability Studies in Britain, and has published numerous books and articles on disability issues.

Mike dedicates this book to his granddaughter Alice Ryall.

Jane dedicates this book to the memory of her husband Graham.

This book is also written in recognition of the dedicated and inspirational efforts of the many disabled people who have died, all too soon and often while at the peak of their powers, in their struggles to bring about the kinds of change we discuss here. You are remembered with pleasure and pride.

Contents

Foreword

This book provides, as yet, the most comprehensive insight into the thinking and tensions that helped create, shape and develop one of the most potentially potent political forces in contemporary British society – the disabled people's movement. Although it has particular relevance to disabled people, students and academics, it will be of interest to anyone and everyone interested in the development of a fairer and more just society.

The potency of the British disabled people's movement can be fully appreciated with reference to the scale and enormity of the structural and cultural forces ranged against it when compared with its achievements. Since at least the nineteenth century, Britain, in common with most western societies, has witnessed the gradual but sustained growth of a multi-billion pound 'disability industry' dependent upon disabled people's continued dependence for its very survival. Many of the organisations which form part of this conglomerate have invested heavily in perpetuating the age-old myth that disabled people are somehow inadequate and, therefore, unable to take their rightful place in mainstream society alongside 'non-disabled' peers. This is only possible because there are no positive representations of disabled people, unlike all other oppressed minorities, within the context of traditional western culture.

Today, there is a flourishing nationwide network of grassroots organisations controlled and run by disabled people. There is a burgeoning 'disability culture' which gives new meaning to notions of 'disability' and a disabled identity. And there are few, including politicians and policy makers, who would not concede that disabled people experience a particularly pervasive form of social oppression or institutional discrimination comparable to that encountered by other marginalised groups such as black people, lesbians and gay men. These are the achievements of the disabled activists and their allies who constitute Britain's disabled people's movement – some of whom have contributed to the production of this book.

But this is not to suggest that the struggle for a non-disabling society is over; far from it. Most of the organisations controlled and run by disabled people survive hand-to-mouth with few, if any, financial resources; the media continue to perpetuate predominantly negative images of people with impairments; and the lifestyle of the overwhelming majority of disabled people is characterised by poverty and social isolation. In addition, recent government policy offers little scope for optimism. The 1993 NHS and community-care reforms represent little more than a reassertion of the traditional, professionally led, individualistic approach to 'disability' management, and the new disability discrimination legislation will do little to remove the numerous environmental and social barriers which confront disabled people. Hence, there is an urgent need to build on what has already been achieved.

It is my firm belief that this book will help facilitate this process, as it has particular relevance to disabled people. This is because it is written by disabled people and it is about disabled people and our struggle for equal rights and opportunities. It is the first book to focus exclusively on the factors, both structural and social, which precipitated the unprecedented growth of self-organisation and political activism among Britain's disabled population. It is also the story of how, in the face of two thousand years of 'conventional' wisdom, disabled people developed and nurtured a range of ideas which have subsequently transformed our understanding of the meaning of disability and, at the same time, generated a sense of pride and collective awareness among the disabled community.

The phenomenal growth of Britain's disabled people's movement can best be appreciated with regard to BCODP – a history of which is provided in this book. BCODP is Britain's national umbrella for organisations controlled and run by disabled people. A founder member of DPI, the international equivalent of the BCODP, it had only seven member organisations at its inaugural meeting in 1981 – the International Year of Disabled People. At the time of writing, September 1995, it has a membership of 108 organisations representing over four hundred thousand disabled individuals. Further, in spite of a perennial and severe lack of financial resources the BCODP has made a significant contribution to disability politics at both the national and international levels. The BCODP campaign for disabled people's rights, for example, has had a major impact on disability organisations throughout Europe.

Yet this apparently meteoric rise to prominence has not been without its problems. Over the years, the BCODP and its member organisations have been criticised on a number of issues by both disabled and non-disabled people. For instance, concern has been expressed over equal opportunities policies with regard to gender, race, sexuality and particular impairments, with reference to the movement's membership and leadership. Given the circumstances in which the movement developed, it is contentious whether such criticisms are justified. But it is to the authors' credit that these and other equally important questions have been explored fully and honestly within this volume.

Besides disabled people this book will also be of interest to students, researchers and academics. This is because the politicisation of disability by disabled people and their organisations has, at last, started to have a major influence in further and higher education. From a practical point of view this is important, because today's students are tomorrow's practitioners and policy makers. What is often referred to as the 'social model of disability' is now an essential component of many courses at the tertiary level. These include medicine and health-related studies, social policy, sociology and cultural studies courses. This approach is evident too in training programmes for teachers, social workers and other professionals. It has also had a major impact on researchers specialising in disability-related research, and on the research establishment. As well as being deeply involved in the disabled people's movement, both Jane (Campbell) and Mike (Oliver), the authors of this book, have made significant contributions to these developments. In the early 1980s Jane was a key figure in the development of 'disability equality training' courses for professionals and practitioners. Mike has written extensively on a whole range of disability-related issues; he is a highly respected academic and theorist, and Britain's first Professor of Disability Studies.

It is ironic, however, that one of the few areas in which this 'new' socio-political approach to disability has yet to make a real impact is political science. This study may help to resolve this situation, as the authors argue that the disabled people's movement is an example of the 'new social movements' which predominate in late capitalist society. Hitherto, the majority of social theorists who have dealt with this particular subject have either ignored disability politics completely or relegated it to the margins of their analysis. Moreover, unlike many of their texts, the argument in this book is not shrouded in unnecessarily obscure and mystifying terminology and jargon. It is written in a refreshingly clear and unambiguous style that relies heavily on the everyday language of the disabled activists who contributed to its production; thus making it accessible to as wide an audience as possible.

For me, this is crucial, because the politics of disablement is about far more than disabled people; it is about challenging oppression in all its forms. Indeed, impairment is not something which is peculiar to a small section of the population; it is fundamental to the human experience. On the other hand, disability – defined by the disabled people's movement as the social oppression of people with impairments – is not. Like racism, sexism, heterosexism and all other forms of social oppression, it is a human creation. It is impossible, therefore, to confront one type of oppression without confronting them all and, of course, the cultural values that created and sustain them. This is why this book will be of particular interest to everyone striving for a future in which any form of social oppression is a thing of the past.

Dr Colin Barnes
School of Sociology and Social Policy
University of Leeds

Acknowledgements

We acknowledge the contribution that all those disabled people we have met over the years have made to this book. Some are included but many are not. We are as grateful to the silent voices of our history as we are to the noisy ones.

In particular Bamber Postance, Colin Barnes, Susan Hemmings and Brenda Joyce made individual contributions which have made the book better than it would otherwise have been.

We thank the Platinum Trust both for a small grant which meant the interviews could be fully transcribed and also for having faith in our work when larger, richer trusts did not.

Cathy Lewington and Joy Oliver undertook the transcription work with speed, precision and care.

Above all, the book could not have been written without the commitment and support of all those who participated and appear in the following pages. We thank them for their participation and, equally important, their trust. We hope we have done justice to their time and commitment and we fully acknowledge that responsibility for shortcomings in the final product is ours.

Abbreviations

ACE	Access Committee for England
ADA	Americans with Disabilities Act
ADAPT	American Disabled People for Attendant Programmes Today
ADL	Anti-discrimination legislation
ADP	Association of Disabled Professionals
AGM	Annual general meeting
BBC	British Broadcasting Corporation
BCODP	British Council of Disabled People (formerly British Council of Organisations of Disabled People)
BDA	British Deaf Association
BSL	British Sign Language
CIL	Centre for integrated/independent living[1]
CORAD	Committee on Restrictions against Disabled People
DA	Disability Alliance
DAA	Disability Awareness in Action
DAIL	*Disability Arts In London* (magazine)
DAN	Direct Action Network
DBC	Disability Benefits Consortium
DCDP	Derbyshire Coalition of Disabled People
DCIL	Derbyshire Centre for Integrated Living
DDA	Disabled Drivers' Association
DHSS	Department of Health and Social Security
DIAL	Disablement Information and Advice Line
DIG	Disablement Income Group
DoH	Department of Health
DPI	Disabled People's International
DRO	Disablement resettlement officer
DSS	Department of Social Security

EEC	European Economic Community
ENIL	European Network on Independent Living
GAD	Greenwich Association of Disabled People
GLAD	Greater London Association of Disabled People
GLC	Greater London Council
HCIL	Hampshire Centre for Independent Living
IL	Independent living
ILF	Independent Living Fund
ILG	Independent Living Group
ILS	Independent Living Scheme
ITV	Independent Television
IYDP	International Year of Disabled People
LA	Local authority
LDAF	London Disability Arts Forum
LEA	Local education authority
LNDP	Liberation Network of Disabled People
LRT	London Regional Transport
MA	Mobility Allowance
MP	Member of Parliament
NFB	National Federation of the Blind
NHS	National Health Service
NLBD	National League of the Blind and Disabled
NUD	National Union of the Deaf
PA	Personal assistance
PSI	Policy Studies Institute
RADAR	Royal Association for Disability and Rehabilitation
RI	Rehabilitation International
RNIB	Royal National Institute for the Blind
RNID	Royal National Institute for the Deaf
SAD	Sisters Against Disablement
SIA	Spinal Injuries Association
TUC	Trades Union Congress
UN	United Nations
UPIAS	Union of the Physically Impaired Against Segregation
VOADL	Voluntary Organisations for Anti-Discrimination Legislation

NOTE

1 In Britain, 'integrated' is used by some organisations and 'independent' by others. The latter is the standard usage in the United States.

Introductions

THE BOOK

This book is a mixture of social theory, political history, action research, individual biography and personal experience. We have resisted the temptation (and some academic advice) to separate out these things and treat them as analytically distinct, because we do not regard them as separable. All of the people in this book are, in our own ways, social theorists, political historians, action researchers and personal autobiographers trying to understand our own experiences. To present all this in separate academic categories is to fly in the face of reality and to distort our own experiences. So each of the chapters which follow will contain a mixture of all those things which make each of us what we are, and as far as possible we will use the words of the people themselves who participated in this project.

The first chapter will set the scene and describe what we did and why we did it in the way we did, and will make explicit our own assumptions on which the work is based. The next chapter will look at the range of services that were put in place after the end of World War II, and the kinds of organisation that were in existence and the experiences of disabled people up to the 1960s. We will suggest that no disability movement, as we will define it here, existed until then but that during that period, the seeds of such a movement were being planted. They were sown by the failure of statutory services to provide disabled people with a decent life, by the failure of existing disability organisations to represent disabled people's real needs and wishes, and by individual disabled people who were beginning to refuse to take it any more.

Chapter 3 will then look at how the foundation stones of the disability movement came to be laid. We will suggest that the movement emerged out of the particular economic and social conditions that existed in Britain in the 1960s and that these produced what we will call the incomes and oppression approaches to disability. Chapter 4 then goes on to look at the specifics of how a small number of organisations controlled and run by disabled people themselves emerged in the 1970s. From these small beginnings, the British Council of Organisations of Disabled People (BCODP, now the British Council of Disabled People) was formed in 1981, and we chart its arrival on the scene.

The next chapter looks at the decade of the 1980s and the struggle of the BCODP to establish itself. As well as considering the influence of the International Year of Disabled People (IYDP) and Disabled People's International (DPI), we look at the way in which the organisation was built and established a credible presence despite chronic underfunding and overt and covert attempts to undermine it. Chapter 6 looks at the impact which the movement has had on transforming the individual and collective consciousness of disabled people. We argue that this developing consciousness is what makes the disability movement 'new', and suggest that while significant strides have been made, there is still a long road to travel.

Chapter 7 looks at some of the issues confronting the movement in the 1990s, most notably how it will successfully incorporate minority groups of disabled people into the broad-based movement. While not minimising the difficulties this may involve, we suggest that the movement has united around the issue of civil rights and that this leads to optimism for the future. Chapter 8 broadens the discussion and looks at the relationships the movement must begin to build with other groups, some within the existing political system and some outside it, as well as considering the vision of a more just and fairer society for disabled people and the kinds of change necessary to achieve it.

Chapter 9 attempts to provide an evaluation of the disability movement, both in terms of the kinds of criterion external analysts of new social movements have suggested, and also in terms of the assessments of disabled people themselves. The final chapter is an interview with the two of us in terms of things we might have wanted to say, had we been interviewees rather than interviewers in constructing the current project. It has enabled us to raise issues not discussed or only partially discussed elsewhere in the text and is in line with our role as active participants in the movement we have been studying.

In order to help the reader to locate what is being said throughout the following chapters, it is necessary that we introduce ourselves and our history. We have placed these biographies at the beginning of the book, rather than at the end in appendices as is customary, because they will provide the framework for interpreting what follows. We do, however, include near the end of the book an annotated glossary which should clarify some of the names used in the text: abbreviations are given in full in the abbreviations list.

OURSELVES

Jane Campbell   When Jane was born in 1959, the doctors told her mother to take her home and enjoy her while she lived – they predicted a life of about a year at the most. As is often the case where named conditions are concerned, they got it wrong, and she is very much alive, chairing the BCODP, which is the national representative voice of the disability movement. During her term of office she has seen the organisation through some of its most pioneering work in the field of independent living, civil rights, peer counselling and equal opportunities. She has been particularly active in creating structures which encourage disabled people from all sectors of society to take control of their lives and influence political and social change. She is currently running a training and project management consultancy in disability rights and independent living (IL).

Mike Oliver   Mike is a disabled academic and political activist. Throughout the last twenty-five years he has tried to combine a political analysis of the experiences of disabled people with a commitment to changing our lives for the better. Originally a 'sporting super-cripple', he got political in the 1970s and his views were shaped by the different experiences he had as a member of the management committees of SKILL and the Spinal Injuries Association (SIA). He became a founding Council member of the BCODP and continues his involvement through its research sub-group. He is a member of the Direct Action Network (DAN) and his ambition (dream?) is to establish a coalition of disabled people in Kent, where he has lived all his life.

BIOGRAPHIES

Simone Aspis   Simone became involved with the disability movement in her mid-twenties when she joined the Integration Alliance. There she discovered her true self in fighting for the end of compulsory segregated education, which she had suffered from herself between the ages of 6 and 16. In 1992 Simone became an assistant with the BBC Radio 4 programme *Does He Take Sugar?*, but, fed up, she decided to take a more proactive role, becoming People First's Parliamentary and Campaigners Officer. She re-wrote the parliamentary bill Civil Rights (Disabled Persons) in pictorial and simple text format so that people with learning difficulties had access to its content. Simone is now 26 and has a dream of using her skills and experience to help the BCODP get full civil rights legislation which is enforceable and accessible for all disabled people. She would also love to see no special schools and no discrimination on the grounds of disability.

Michael Barrett   Mike was educated at the Birmingham Royal Institute for the Blind. He entered segregated workshops at 16 years of age, and was trained in bedding and upholstery. He transferred to the General Welfare of the Blind, London, where he qualified as instructor of the blind. He was promoted to Foreman and then to General Works Manager. In 1979 Mike became General Secretary of the National League of the Blind and Disabled (NLBD). He has served on many committees concerning the employment of disabled people, especially as an active trade unionist. In 1993 he was elected UK representative to the European Disability Forum HELIOS II programme. He has recently retired.

Elsa Beckett   Elsa was born and brought up in central Africa. Her main occupation is creative writing concerning disability. Elsa first became involved in the disability movement as a co-founder of GEMMA, the national friendship and support group of disabled lesbians and bisexual women, which in its turn was one of the founding members of the BCODP. Elsa feels her greatest achievement has been maintaining the GEMMA network and newsletter despite having no charitable trust or local authority (LA) funding. Her work with disabled women has been her best pleasure.

Nasa Begum   Nasa has been actively involved in the disability movement for several years, and has been chair of Waltham Forest Association of Disabled People and Powerhouse. She has written extensively around simultaneous oppression, and as a black disabled woman is involved in race, gender and disability politics. Nasa is currently employed as a Research Fellow at PSI. Before that she worked at the Kings Fund Centre promoting the involvement of disabled people in planning, implementing and evaluating services. Nasa's background is in research, training, policy development and social work.

Stephen Bradshaw   Stephen was born in 1941 and entered marketing and technical sales in the UK and Europe after studying printing at college. His first involvement with an organisation funded and controlled by disabled people was with the Disablement Income Group (DIG) in 1968. He was also a founder member of the BCODP and its longest-serving National Council member. He was involved in the development of SIA from one staff member in 1977 to an organisation with over thirty staff, and helped similar organisations start in other countries. He is currently SIA Executive Director and Chair of Rights Now, the UK coalition of organisations of and for disabled people campaigning for anti-discrimination legislation (ADL).

Ken Davis   Ken became convinced of the need for disabled people to unite in our own organisations though his contribution to the Union of the Physically Impaired Against Segregation (UPIAS) in the early 1970s. Since then, he has worked to motivate and organise the active participation of disabled people in a number of other groups, including the Derbyshire Coalition of Disabled People (DCDP) and the Derbyshire Centre for Independent Living (CIL). Ken currently gives background support to local disability organisations, seeking to encourage more recent members of the movement to carry forward the struggle for control over our own lives and affairs.

Maggie Davis   Maggie was institutionalised for ten years during the 1960s and 1970s in segregated residential homes and was a leading figure in the early struggles by residents against oppressive institutional regimes. These experiences later found political expression through her involvement in the formation of UPIAS. Maggie escaped from institutional 'care' by campaigning and working with other disabled people on the design and provision of a housing collective under the operational control of its tenants. This experience, in the period before there were any community services or independent living provisions, added to the insights that Maggie took into her membership of DCDP and the Derbyshire CIL. She is currently an active member of both, offering peer support and counselling to other disabled people and representing the interests of disabled people in a number of mainstream agencies and organisations.

John Evans   John first became involved in the disability movement in the early 1980s when he was both trying individually to establish his own independent living scheme (ILS) and involved collectively with other disabled people in founding the Hampshire Centre for Independent Living (HCIL). His main areas of involvement have been around IL issues and training and in the setting up and running of organisations of disabled people. John has been involved with the BCODP since 1987 in a number of different roles as well as in the capacity of Chair. He also sits on the board of the European Network on Independent Living (ENIL) and was in Strasbourg in 1989 when the ENIL resolutions were adopted by disabled people in Europe. As far as the future is concerned, he wants no less than to see our long campaigns for equal rights and direct payments legislation enshrined in law and, actively through ENIL, to see IL initiatives, schemes and policy develop throughout southern, central and eastern Europe.

Vic Finkelstein   Vic's involvement in the disability movement has its origins with a spinal injury during a school sports activity in South Africa. Since then he has used a wheelchair. Following his imprisonment and banishment for his opposition to apartheid, he left his South African home in 1968 as a political exile. In 1975, after completing a teacher training course, Vic joined the Open University to work on the 'Handicapped Person in the Community' course. This was perhaps the first course in what has now become 'disability studies'. Currently a Senior Lecturer in the School of Health and Social Welfare, Vic has contributed to several courses concerned with the development of the social interpretation of disability. One of his well-known achievements in the disability movement was being one of the prime originators of the social interpretation of disability alongside the formation of several organisations of disabled people, including UPIAS and the BCODP, of which he was the first Chair. He represented the UK on the first World Council of DPI for the first five years after its formation.

Joe Hennessey Joe became involved in disability issues when he joined the Invalid Tricycle Association (now the Disabled Drivers' Association (DDA)) in 1959. He has served on its governing body (by constitution all members have to be disabled people) continuously since 1963, including three terms as National Chairman. As part of a campaign for better mobility provision by government, Joe chaired a mass protest rally in Trafalgar Square in 1971 and led a delegation to meet Prime Minister Ted Heath afterwards. Joe served on the BCODP Council in its early years. He was appointed a Governor of Motability in 1977 and was a Trustee of the Independent Living Fund (ILF) between 1988 and 1993.

David Hevey David is a writer, photographer and broadcaster. He became disabled when 15 years old. At the time, he states, his impairment – epilepsy – brought both psychological and physical chaos. He went to college, became an artist, and developed his socialist credentials: as he puts it, 'I realised working-class people could and did affect the world.' However, his impairment, although termed 'hidden' by others, caused him to continue to see himself as a 'desperate outsider'. Meeting the disabled people's movement dissolved his 'terror, fear and loneliness'. Initially as a photographer, and more lately as a programme maker, he has been at the forefront of the debate concerning the representation of disabled people. His unique combination of analysis and technical skills has enabled him to challenge notions of the 'positive image'. He lives with his partner and their 1-year-old son in central London.

Millidrette Hill　Millie is the co-founder of the Black Disabled People's Association established in 1990. Having travelled extensively doing a combined honours degree in politics and economics at York University, Toronto, and then a Masters Degree from the New York Institute of Technology, Millie has now settled in the UK, where she is a student barrister and researcher/writer in race and disability issues. Millie was born in Bermuda where, at the age of 14, she became disabled as a result of a diving accident. Four years later she helped to set up the island's first organisation of disabled people. She was actively involved in the disability movements of both the United States and Canada. She became involved in the disability movement in Britain out of her concern for the extreme marginalisation of black disabled people within both mainstream society and the disabled communities.

Alan Holdsworth (a.k.a. Johnny Crescendo)　Alan 'The Hat' Holdsworth is famous – or perhaps notorious – for his multi-coloured cap. He is always one of the first to be picked out for arrest on any action. Alan is DAN's National Organiser and one of its founding members. He has co-ordinated all DAN's national actions from Christchurch to Cardiff, and in this role he supports disabled people campaigning for civil rights in their own areas. He was at the forefront of the current wave of radical action when, in 1988 with a few others, he transformed a polite but ineffectual protest against pedestrianisation in Chesterfield, Derbyshire, into a campaign of civil disobedience: disabled people won and the rest is making history. Alan was key in organisations like the successful Block Telethon and now DAN, which has representatives in most British cities (so nowhere is safe). Alan's involvement in the disabled people's movement began in the 1980s, when he was a youth worker running a project for people with learning difficulties. He helped them to 'fly over the cuckoo's nest' and in the process wrote the song 'Choices and Rights', which he has performed (as Johnny Crescendo, singer/songwriter) all over Europe and North America and which has become widely regarded as the 'anthem' of the international disability movement.

Judith Hunt　Judy's first 'awakenings' around the politics of disablement came from her work at Le Court in 1963. She became a close ally to a group of residents who were emerging from a long, bitter struggle against the oppressive regime of the institutional culture of the time. It was here she learnt that disability was much more than a physical limitation. Her mentor on the burning issue was a resident, Paul Hunt, who later became her husband. Judith attributes her continued learning to participating alongside Paul in the struggles of disabled people for liberation and equality of opportunity, which she witnessed, and she shared in the development of UPIAS.

Rachel Hurst Rachel is currently Director of Disability Awareness in Action (DAA), an international public education organisation, which was established in 1992 to further the human rights of all disabled people in accordance with the United Nations (UN) World Programme of Action concerning Disabled Persons (1982). Rachel has been active in DPI since its inception in 1981, currently holding the position of Chair of the European Regional Committee. In the UK, she chaired the BCODP (1985–7), and was a founding member of one of the first CILs in Greenwich. She has been at the forefront of the disability movement since the early 1980s.

Paddy Ladd Paddy was born deaf in 1952, and was one of the first to be assimilated into the hearing education system. After being rescued from this miserable fate, he became a community activist. He has always been a maverick. Initially he became a social worker with deaf children and their families for three years, but, horrified by what he saw in those families and schools (where sign language was forbidden by medical edict), he joined with other deaf people to co-found a pressure group, the National Union of the Deaf (NUD), in 1976. A similar activist path led him to work for *See Hear*, the BBC's deaf programme, which the NUD had helped establish. After three years of trying to change attitudes there, he admitted defeat, leaving to found the London Deaf Video Project, which enabled deaf people to record their own language and culture, fight for government recognition of that language, and try to reforge links between deaf 'grassroots' people and the emerging deaf elite. He continues to fight for a deaf-centred deaf education system, and for deaf schools, which have become endangered by disability rights activities. Although he emphasises that deaf people are a linguistic minority, he advocates working as a coalition with disabled people, whose issues he strongly identifies with. At present he is pursuing a PhD in deaf culture, because of the lack both of deaf academics and of understanding of the subject in question. For light relief, he works as a signer at Grateful Dead concerts, and on signed songs which reflect deaf experience.

Barbara Lisicki (a.k.a. Wanda Barbara) Socialist, feminist and long-term (but not lifelong) disabled person, formerly a person with a disability but now a stroppy crip, Barbara helped to found the Campaign to Stop Patronage in the late 1980s and early 1990s. This targeted charity beanfeasts like Children in Need and ITV's Telethon, organising the successful one-off Block Telethon (in 1992) with a demonstration of a thousand plus of the 'ungrateful disabled' (the *Guardian*'s description) and contributing to Telethon's demise. In 1993 she helped to set up DAN, and is responsible for its press and publicity. She owns twenty-five pairs of handcuffs (but London Regional Transport has thousands of buses!) and has been arrested in several major British cities. She has also avoided arrest in several American cities whilst attending American Disabled People for Attendant Programmes Today (ADAPT) actions, but learned a lot from ADAPT about the strategy and tactics of non-violent direct action. Barbara's other persona is Wanda Barbara, stand-up comic since 1988, given her first 'break' by Mr Arden, orthopaedic surgeon, and then by the London Disability Arts Forum (LDAF) in which she is still involved. She makes a living tormenting – sorry, training – social workers and making fun of the able-bodied.

Colin Low After teaching law and criminology at Leeds University for sixteen years, Colin Low became Director of the Disability Resource Team, a post which he held from 1984 to 1994, during which time he took it from the Greater London Council (GLC) to independent charitable status. He is now a Senior Research Fellow at City University Rehabilitation Resource Centre, where he is carrying out research on the social model of disability. Throughout all this time, he has been active in a wide range of organisations concerned with blindness and disability. In the 1970s he helped to found the Association of Blind and Partially Sighted Teachers and Students, SKILL and the Disability Alliance (DA). He served on the Executive Council of the National Federation of the Blind (NFB) between 1969 and

1992, holding all the major offices within the organisation and serving as President from 1979 to 1982. Again in the 1970s he was a member of Lord Snowdon's 'working party on the integration of the disabled', where he was one of the first to recommend the introduction of ADL on grounds of disability in this country. He has served on the executive council of the Royal National Institute for the Blind (RNIB) since 1975 and been its vice-chair since 1990.

Ann MacFarlane MBE   Ann is self-employed as a disability equality training consultant and researcher. She has recently completed a housing and community-care research project for the BCODP. Ann's involvement in the disability movement took off in 1984 when she helped turn her traditional local disability organisation into a body controlled by disabled people. She then took lessons learnt from that experience to develop peer counselling and empowerment courses for disabled people.

Micheline Mason   Micheline was co-founder of the Liberation Network of Disabled People (LNDP) and editor of the first newspaper, *In from the Cold*, for and by disabled people only. In 1995 Micheline is the proud single parent of an 11-year-old disabled daughter, Lucy, and one of the UK's leading activists campaigning for fully inclusive education. In this role Micheline chairs the Integration Alliance, which supports parents fighting to get their disabled children into mainstream schools. On becoming a parent Micheline realised that the moves forward she and other disabled adults had made had not touched the lives of disabled children. To her the special school system was an anachronism, yet on behalf of her daughter, she found herself 'dragged back into the same old battles' she had left behind her. Micheline is dedicated to getting educationalists and the general public to embrace full equality for disabled children in all establishments.

Phillip Mason   Phil joined the ranks of disabled people as the result of an accident in 1972. Following treatment, he went to live in a residential home in the south of England. In the late 1970s he became involved with a group of fellow residents who were determined that they did not want to spend the rest of their lives 'in the Home'. They wanted to live in the community 'like everyone else'. Through research, mutual support and local campaigning, the group persuaded the LA and housing authorities to take their initiative seriously. It was the group's argument that the money being used to pay for their support in the Home could be given to them to enable them to buy and organise their own support in the community. Eventually this was accepted by the local authority. Success came and all those involved moved into their own homes. Out of these simple beginnings, two things emerged. First, the local authority decided to build on the success of the scheme. Second, the group decided to keep together and form HCIL, a local organisation of disabled people promoting and supporting independent living. Subsequently members of the group became active both nationally and internationally.

Jenny Morris   Jenny's involvement in disability politics flowed naturally from her identity as a socialist and feminist. In writing *Pride Against Prejudice: Transforming Attitudes to Disability*, she attempted to raise awareness of the discrimination and oppression disabled women face. Jenny has just finished editing a collection of writing by disabled women entitled *Feminism and Disability*, to be published by the Women's Press.

Elspeth Morrison   Elspeth has had an impairment since birth, and after spending much of her childhood in hospital, she concluded there was nothing positive about being a disabled person. Fortuitously, at the age of 23, she met other disabled people at a writing workshop, who cheerily pointed out she was 'one of them', turning her sense of self around. Since then she has been a leading exponent of disability arts, as both writer and performer. For six years she was editor of *Disability Arts in London* (*DAIL*) magazine, until moving into television production, where she is currently a producer at the BBC's Disability Programme Unit. Although a skilful producer of factual programmes, she is happiest writing and directing comedy; her latest project is directing a disabled woman's theatre company called No Excuses. Her advice is regularly sought by the mainstream arts world and she has written a number of publications for the Arts Council. She is Chair of Graeae Theatre Company and lives in West London.

Alan Pinn   Alan has defied his medical prognosis of fifteen years to live – given by the medical profession when he was 10, because of his duchanne muscular dystrophy – so far by some thirty-four years. He is currently Chair of the Board of Volunteer Directors (all disabled) running Ashwellthorpe Hall Hotel in Norfolk, a unique hotel accessible to all disabled people and their families, partners and friends. Alan's main entry into the disability movement was joining the DDA in 1961 when driving his first invalid tricycle; he became involved in campaigning against the introduction of parking meters in Kingston because of the restrictions it would impose on disabled people. He was one of the delegation of DDA members who gave evidence to the Baroness Sharp inquiry on the vehicle needs of disabled people. He assisted with the organisation of a mass lobby of Parliament on the mobility issue. His most pleasing achievement is seeing the standing that Richmond Advice and Information on Disability has today, being the only founder member still active in the organisation.

Anne Rae   Anne has been active and interested in disability issues for over twenty years. As the BCODP Secretary, Treasurer and later Development Worker, she has been key in the development of the organisation's structure and outreach programme. Anne has also been very keen to organise on a local level, founding both the Barnet Independent Disability Action group and Disabled Women in Greenwich. Anne's passion for the arts resulted in her co-founding LDAF. When she moved to Manchester she became Chair of the Disability Arts Advisory Group to the Board of Directors of Manchester City of Drama.

Patricia J. Rock   Patricia is currently Chair of the BCODP Women's Group and Co-Chair of DPI's European Disabled Women's Committee. Patricia has been active, for many years, in both the disability movement and the women's movement. She is currently writing her doctoral thesis on the invisibility of disabled women in society, and is the editor of the first 'Global Report on the Rights and Demands of Disabled Women' (due to be published shortly). Patricia is also an artist and incorporates her interests in women and disability in her work. She has exhibited four times both here and in mainland Europe. She has also run art workshops for disabled people and children from war zones.

Sian Vasey Sian's involvement with the disability movement has been primarily with disability arts. She was involved in setting up LDAF and *DAIL* magazine in 1986 and the National Disability Arts Forum in 1990, and she continues to serve on the committees of both organisations. She also has a longstanding involvement with Graeae Theatre Company and has worked in disability television since 1987, presenting and researching the *LINK* programme. In 1991 she edited *LINK* magazine, and when that folded after six glorious issues, she became a director/presenter on the TV programme. In 1993 she set up Cryptic Productions as a partnership and co-produced a three-part series on the disability charities, *Poor Dear*, for the BBC. She then set up her own company, Circle Pictures, in 1994, and in that guise produced and directed two documentaries for Channel 4, one on disability and motherhood and one on disability and technology.

Rosalie Wilkins Rosalie is a freelance television producer/presenter. She has been involved in disability politics and information services since leaving university, where she became a wheelchair user in 1966. Her apprenticeship in disability politics began with DIG and – by contrast – working for the Central Council for the Disabled (now RADAR), where she started the information bulletin. Her involvement in television came with a World in Action programme about a Dutch disabled village in 1972. This led to the producer, Richard Creasey, joining forces with Rosalie to pioneer *LINK*, the first radical and unique programme to give voice to the emerging disability movement. Rosalie went on to produce highly successful mainstream documentaries portraying the movement's struggle both nationally and internationally; amongst the best were *We Won't Go Away*, *Statement of Intent* and *Circling the Dragon*.

Richard Wood In 1990 Richard became the first ever Director of the BCODP. His apprenticeship in the disability movement began when he left a financial management career in industry to take time out at university. During that time he met disabled activists like Ken Davis, who inspired him to put his energies into establishing the UK's first CIL in Derbyshire. Richard subsequently became Director of the CIL. Throughout the BCODP's evolution, Richard has believed that the greatest issue facing disabled people is the systematic abuse of our civil and human rights. As a result of this he is currently working with Disabled Peoples International to establish an Amnesty-type organisation to monitor and report on human rights violations against disabled people.

HISTORICAL LANDMARKS

1890   British Deaf Association (BDA) formed.

1899   National League of the Blind formed as a trade union.

1902   National League of the Blind affiliated to Trades Union Congress (TUC).

1920   Blind workers march to London from all over Britain to protest against low wages and poor working conditions.

1933   Blind workers march to London again.

1947   DDA formed.

1965   Formation of DIG.

1970   Chronically Sick and Disabled Persons Act.

1972   UPIAS formed.

1974   SIA established.

1975   United Nations Declaration of the Rights of Disabled Persons.

1976   'Fundamental Principles of Disability' document (UPIAS 1976) published.

1976   *LINK*'s first broadcast.

1977   Project 81 started at Le Court in Hampshire.

1979   LNDP formed.

1981   International Year of Disabled People.

1981   Britain's first coalition of disabled people established in Derbyshire.

1981   BCODP steering group established.

1981   DPI formed. First World Congress held in Singapore.

1982   Full constitution ratified at inaugural meeting of BCODP.

1982   First attempt to introduce ADL bill. Introduced by Jack Ashley MP.

1982   Committee on Restrictions against Disabled People (CORAD) issued report giving evidence of over seven hundred cases of discrimination and recommending ADL.

1982   UN World Programme of Action concerning Disabled People adopted.

1983	UN General Assembly proclaimed a Decade of Disabled Persons to 1992.
1985	DPI Second World Congress held in Bahamas.
1986	Disabled Persons (Services, Consultation and Representation) Act.
1988	'Rights Not Charity' march in London.
1990	Americans with Disabilities Act (ADA) passed.
1991	BCODP published the first case for fully comprehensive ADL.
1992	DPI Third World Congress held in Vancouver.
1993	DAN formed after its first 'action' in Christchurch.
1994	DPI Fourth World Congress held in Sydney.
1995	Fourteenth attempt to introduce ADL (failed at second reading).
1995	BCODP admits individual members and changes its name to the British Council of Disabled People.
1995	Disability Discrimination Act passed despite opposition from the disability movement.

Chapter 1

Setting the scene

Social movements can be viewed as collective enterprises to establish a new order of life.

(Blumer 1995: 60)

WHERE TO BEGIN?

At the outset it is important to say what this book is not. It is not a history of disability. It is not the history of the disability movement. Both of these projects may, one day, materialise; but, because of the neglect of the lives and experiences of disabled people, the former is not yet feasible; and as far as the latter is concerned, while we are clear about what constitutes the disability movement, others are less sure, or not sure if it is a movement at all.

Our intention is much simpler than that; it is to present a series of perspectives on the process of self-organisation of disabled people that has been occurring over the last thirty years. If the book has a rationale at all, it is captured in the words of deaf activist Paddy Ladd, when he responded to our request to be involved in the project:

the process of freeing ourselves from imposed histories is in itself a historical and dialectical process. In these new and exciting times, whatever you or I set down are merely the first steps on the road to a full and comprehensive history of not just the disability movement as a whole, but of all its constituent parts of each particular disability group.

All projects or histories have to start somewhere after the dawn of time, the big bang or the coupling of Adam and Eve. We have chosen to start somewhere around thirty years ago, although we fully acknowledge and recognise the fact that some disabled people were self-organising long before that. Indeed, some of the contributors to the project have made this point crystal clear. Phillip Mason, who has been active in the independent living (IL) movement for many years, suggests that disabled people have always been involved in collective self-organisation:

> I think there's always been a disability movement. I don't think, necessarily, it's ever regarded itself as a disability movement but the struggles that we identify with today may be the struggles individuals or perhaps groups have always identified with in the past. Although perhaps they focused on different issues in their day, nevertheless groups of oppressed people, which is the language that we use now but perhaps wasn't the language that was used in those days, always existed and always strove for the sort of things that we would recognise. I think that's always gone on and perhaps to call it a disability movement is stretching a point but, nevertheless, we should recognise that the spirit of what's going on today always existed. It's always been human nature to want more personal autonomy, to want to have more control over what happens in one's own life. There's nothing peculiar about what's going on today, it's always been there. Perhaps we're fortunate today in that it's at last found a route, it's at last begun to be recognised by the population at large.

Mason not only takes us to task for our historical short-sightedness but also raises the question of what constitutes a movement. Judy Hunt, a long-term ally of the movement and widow of the late Paul Hunt, has herself studied the history and development of the disability movement. Paul was one of the first disabled people to confront segregation and institutionalisation as a form of oppression, by organising disabled people incarcerated in homes either to 'take over the management' or to 'break out'. She draws attention to the way the movement has evolved historically and relates this to other social movements:

> My understanding of the movement is that you get a lot of protest activity going on; bits and pieces here and there and you can go right back into the nineteenth century and see bits of protest, but does that constitute a movement? Some people might say that is the beginning of a movement. Whereas recent

studies of other social movements tend to look at how they become much more developed, how they enthuse society much more, how they filter through. It's not just small groups here and there; it actually begins to have an impact much more broadly. And studying the history of the disability movement is like trying to put together the jigsaw puzzle of that process. At what point or what points do you decide that certain key developments, with hindsight, were influential?

Here Hunt is drawing attention to the distinction that sociologists, who have studied social movements, draw between emergent and mature social movements. This process of transformation from an emergent to a mature movement is, we would suggest, precisely the point at which we are writing this book about the disability movement.

But there is an earlier question that also needs to be addressed: 'In the long history and theorizing about social movements, no question has received more attention than that concerning the origin of social movements. What factors make for a movement in the first place?' (Marx and McAdam 1994: 77). This is a question we will be addressing in subsequent chapters, but here we need to make clear why we started where we did, why we consider disabled people's attempt at self-organisation to be a movement, how we undertook the work and why we chose to carry it out in the way we did.

WHY WE STARTED WHERE WE DID

The decade of the 1980s saw a transformation in our understandings of disability. In consequence, and in order to ensure the full economic and social integration of disabled people, as required by the United Nations Declaration of the Rights of Disabled Persons (1975), the kinds of policy and service have changed. Section 3447.12 of this Declaration asserts: 'organisations of disabled persons may be usefully consulted in all matters regarding the rights of disabled persons'.

At the heart of this was the rise in the number of organisations controlled and run by disabled people themselves. At the beginning of the decade there were very few such organisations, but by 1990 there was an international organisation known as Disabled People's International (DPI) and a national co-ordinating body,

ish Council of Organisations of Disabled People (BCODP).
time the BCODP's constituent organisations had risen to
hundred, most of which were local coalitions of disabled
people or centres for integrated living (CILs).

By any standards this numerical growth was remarkable, but
there are four reasons why it was even more remarkable than
appears at first sight. First, all organisations controlled by
disabled people suffered from chronic underfunding throughout
the decade, even from national and international agencies which
are supposed to support such developments. Second, many
politicians, policy makers and professionals had no faith in the
viability of a new movement which was being built by people
who had so far seemed passive and dependent. Third, the new
movement was built in the teeth of opposition from the traditional
voluntary organisations which, up to now, had been in control of
disability; and this opposition was often active rather than
passive. Finally, because of the disabling environments that
disabled people encounter, the difficulties involved in simply
finding ways to meet, communicate and organise should not be
underestimated.

This growth was not merely a numerical phenomenon, but also
reflected the individual and collective empowerment of disabled
people through the organisations they were creating. This can be
seen in a number of ways. It can be seen in the challenge to
dominant social perceptions of disability as personal tragedy and
the affirmation of positive images of disability through the
development of a politics of personal identity. It can be also be
seen in the development and articulation of the social model of
disability, which, by focusing on disabling environments rather
than individual impairments, freed up disabled people's hearts
and minds by offering an alternative conceptualisation of the
problem. Liberated, the direction of disabled people's personal
energies turned outwards to building a force for changing society.
The social model vehicle has been fundamental in carrying the
movement forward at such a rapid pace. Finally, it can be seen in
the numbers of disabled people literally taking to the streets, not
only as a form of social protest but in pursuit of their everyday
lives.

The origins of these fundamental changes, it seems to us, can be
found in the 1960s with the coming of the 'age of affluence', when
disabled people began to organise around issues of income,

employment, rights and community living rather than institutional care. It continued in the 1970s with the passage of the Chronically Sick and Disabled Persons Act (1970) and the formation of the Union of the Physically Impaired Against Segregation (UPIAS). It culminated in the 1980s with the events already described.

WHY DOES THIS CONSTITUTE A SOCIAL MOVEMENT?

There is a need to describe, chart and analyse all this, not simply because a remarkable decade of activity needs to be captured and recorded, although of course the history of disability as seen by disabled people is important in its own right. But more than that, the decade of the 1980s saw a range of new social movements develop, from environmentalism and the green movement, through the challenges to social oppression by groups such as women, black people and gays and lesbians, and on to a resurgence of the peace movement.

These new movements differed radically from older ones which had tended to campaign on single issues, were led by experts and saw parliamentary lobbying as their only tactic. The new movements were much more concerned with a broad range of issues, were populist and used a variety of tactics. Providing a precise definition of the disability movement is no easy task, but Barbara Lisicki, a prominent member of the Direct Action Network (DAN), comes nearest to our own definition:

> I don't think anyone knows for sure what a movement is but essentially what we are talking about is a set of ideas and an analysis which people can then support in different ways. I always think of the movement as a set of people that have somehow made a connection with a set of ideas. The disability movement is obviously a set of ideas that presents a challenge to dominant ideology that says disabled people are burdens on society and that they should be taken care of but the disability movement is also about people who believe that they have right to a life.

A case study of one such movement will throw light on the politics of the 1980s and offer insights into future political developments on into the twenty-first century. There is also a not-so-hidden agenda for us in writing this book. In the vast majority of other studies and analyses of new social movements, the struggles of disabled people barely get a mention, and even when they do, the authors tend to use the category 'the disabled' or even 'the handicapped' in an almost throw-away manner that indicates that they know nothing and care little about our struggles.

In earlier writings one of us (Oliver and Zarb 1989; Oliver 1990) argued that the formation of these organisations controlled and run by disabled people constituted a movement, and that collectively these organisations exhibited the characteristics of new social movements. In a recent paper, disabled activist Ken Davis (1993) not only describes the history of what he calls 'the disability movement' but supports our claims that it constitutes what social theorists would call a new social movement.

The reasons for this are, at one level, very simple, for: 'Social movements can be defined as organised efforts to promote or resist change in society that rely, at least in part, on non-institutionalised forms of political action' (Marx and McAdam 1994: 3). Clearly the purpose of disabled people's self-organisation is to promote change: to improve the quality of our lives and promote our full inclusion into society. It does this both through involvement in the formal political system and through the promotion of other kinds of political activity.

The definitional issues surrounding new social movements are more complex than this (for extended discussion, see Oliver 1995: Ch. 10), and we will return to them later. However, here we need to make clear that our definition of the disability movement focuses on those organisations democratically controlled and run by disabled people themselves. It does not include those traditional voluntary organisations and charities that are not run by disabled people.

Throughout the book we will use the term 'the disability movement' rather than the alternative 'the disabled people's movement' because the former is the term used by most members of the movement itself. The latter term may gain increasing currency over the next few years because it clearly demarcates between those organisations controlled by disabled people and those not. Even though some may use the term 'the disability movement' to include non-democratic and non-accountable organisations, we state clearly here that we exclude those organisations from our definition used throughout this book.

Thus, for us, the disability movement is a new social movement in that it is beginning to offer disabled people a democratic and political voice; something we have never had before. In similar ways, other new social movements are offering other disenfranchised groups a voice where they were previously silent. So our intention is to write a book which will be a case study of the rise of the disability movement and to locate this within discussions of new social movements in general and their effects on the changing nature of politics in the late twentieth century.

Not everyone who participated in this project was in agreement with our focus. Colin Low provides the most articulate criticism:

> First of all, one or two points about the central focus of the project, which I think requires some re-emphasis if it is to do full justice to historical reality. Your proposal paper reads as if the disability movement owes its origins to the developments of the 1980s. This does not take sufficient account of the great amount of activity undertaken before that time by organisations such as the National League of the Blind and the British Deaf Association, which dates back to the 1890s, and the National Federation of the Blind which was founded in 1947. Nor I think should one lose sight of the contribution of the Disablement Income Group from the mid-60s. Simply confining myself to things which are within my own knowledge, these organisations undertook an enormous amount of self-organisation, representation, lobbying, agitation and general development of a disability consciousness. Perhaps the most outstanding illustration of this is the agitation of the National League of the Blind which led to the passing of the Blind Persons Acts of 1920 and 1938.

So far little has been written on this specific topic except for a brief discussion of the origins of the disability movement (Pagel 1988), the development (Oliver 1984) and refinement (Oliver 1990) of a framework to analyse the rise of disability organisations and their relationship to traditional voluntary organisations, and a case study of international aspects of the movement (Driedger 1989). More recently, Davis and Mullender (1993) have described the rise of a local coalition of disabled people. We hope, therefore, that this book will be a contribution to this literature and offer a path for disabled people not just to take control of our current lives but also to reclaim our own history.

HOW WE APPROACHED THE WORK

Our attempts to produce this book reflect an inherent tension in much social research: that between insider and outsider accounts. We are both insiders in the disability movement, although, obviously, our individual relationships to this movement are very different. We have provided brief biographies of ourselves and the other participants in this study (see 'Introductions') to enable the reader to contextualise the accounts we provide.

We should make it clear that, therefore, we are unashamedly attempting to provide an insider account of the rise of the disability movement as we define it. Until now, with the notable exceptions of Touraine (1981) and Altman (1994), there have been few insider accounts of the dynamics of emerging social movements, partly because: 'the study of movements in process cannot be readily separated from a research relationship that approximates an act of intervention' (Morrow 1994: 298–9). The approaches underpinning the accounts of Touraine and Altman are explicitly sociological, foregrounding sociological ideas and using both the development of the French Communist Party and collective responses to AIDS as the substantive area in which to test these ideas. We are more concerned to foreground a description of the emerging disability movement, and sociological (and indeed, non-sociological) ideas are relevant when they enable us to make sense of events we are describing or to clarify issues we are discussing. We approach the research task as activists trying to make sense of our actions, not as researchers trying to be where the action is.

As well as being an insider account, this is also a partisan one in the sense that we have not attempted to be 'objective', whatever that may mean. Altman claims that:

> AIDS-related research has broken down the pretence of 'objectivity' among social researchers, for AIDS has prodded a number of behavioural and social scientists into an autobiographical exercise in self-reflection. This is most evident in the case of gay men, many of whom found in the epidemic the opportunity to combine the personal – namely their own participation in the gay community, their own anxieties, griefs and fears around the epidemic – with the professional, namely their skills in medical, social and behavioural research.
>
> (Altman 1994: 128)

While finding little else that we agree with in a recent book on 'the management of normality', we find the author's discussion of the relationship of the research process to the researcher mirrors our own position in relation to this project:

> There is no vantage point outside the human community, no privileged position from which to observe it: one may at best disentangle oneself, but one can never be disconnected. An observer may be a bit more detached but even that stance in itself is not sufficient for understanding. Insight requires at one level reflexive detachment, and at other levels involvement. In order to understand how people relate to one another and themselves, empathic involvement is required. In order to explain these relations as part of a wider figuration, one needs analytic detachment.
>
> (De Swaan 1990: 6)

While we want to point out that other groups have also played a key role in breaking down the barriers of objective research, for us this current book is an attempt to combine the personal with the political and to locate this in our own history.

HOW WE CARRIED OUT THE WORK

In writing this book there were three main methods for gathering the information on which it is based and which utilise our insider status:

(a) the scrutiny and analysis of documentary sources, including minutes and papers from the BCODP and discussions and descriptions which have appeared in the new disability journals that have risen in conjunction with the new movement;
(b) in-depth interviews with twenty-three disabled people who have been centrally involved in the events described above;
(c) our own perceptions and understandings, as we have been active participants ourselves in the history and contemporary struggles discussed here.

There are a number of other points that need to be made about this. To begin with, as we have been key participants in the events and experiences described below, the book is based upon the ethnographic and action research traditions. Without entering into disputes about what constitutes action research, the following definition reflects our own stance:

> Action research is a form of collective, self-reflective inquiry undertaken by participants in social situations in order to improve the rationality and justice of their own social or educational practices, as well as their understanding of these practices and the situations in which these practices are carried out.
>
> (Kemmis and McTaggart 1988: 5)

We recognise that many disabled people are suspicious of research (Oliver 1992; Morris 1992; Woodwill 1993), and we encountered this reaction when setting the project up. However, in conceptualising research as collective, self-reflective inquiry, we hope that some of these suspicions can be addressed. The following quotation captures our own position: 'The use of self – the influence/impact of self – plays an important part in the unfolding of multiple realities. In this sense, research becomes part of a shared enterprise or a joint search for truth; a co-production of knowledge' (Atkinson and Shakespeare 1993: 6).

WHY WE CARRIED OUT THE WORK IN THE WAY WE DID

In writing about our own collective history, we also recognise that our approach is in line with the demands of other groups, such as women and black people, to write their own histories and define their own issues. In beginning the process of producing our own history, we hope the work will neither only be faithfully descriptive of our experience (ethnography), nor merely serve as a platform for internal developments within the movement (action research), but will also make a genuine, if small, contribution to our liberation. If it does, then post hoc the research will be seen to have been emancipatory (Oliver 1992).

We have had few problems with access to information or people to interview, for the disability movement has long recognised the need for research of this kind. As we have already stated, our main source of information has been ourselves and other disabled people engaged in the struggle to improve the lives of all disabled people.

In choosing the people to interview, we did not use random,

quota, snowball or any other form of sampling. Instead we contacted people who we knew would have useful things to tell us. Inevitably we were not able to interview everyone we would have liked to, but we hope our choice does justice to the silent many as well as the vocal few. Most of those contacted agreed to be interviewed, a few refused for a variety of reasons, and some sent written comments instead. We do not claim, therefore, that what follows is an objective account of our recent history, but it is a description and analysis of some of the issues that face us as we continue our collective struggle for self-organisation and empowerment.

In what follows, we try to use what people told us in their own words, as far as possible. All the interviews we carried out were fully transcribed, read by both of us and put into a structure that we decided upon. We used a semi-structured interview schedule which focused initially on the genesis and development of the disability movement, particularly as it emerged in the 1960s and 1970s. We then focused on an analysis and discussion of the developments throughout the 1980s, especially in respect of the emergence and development of the BCODP. Finally, we talked about future developments in the movement as well as more general developments in politics, policy and service provision.

Not everyone discussed each of these issues in equal depth or at all, and in some cases different interpretations of the same events were proffered. We have attempted to show these different, if not at times contradictory, recollections of particular events, discussions or policies. These varied interpretations give an important indication of the many creative tensions that have been characteristic of the movement.

This then has been an account of the way the work proceeded and why we carried it out in the ways we did, and a discussion of the assumptions which underpin it. What now follows is the work itself.

Chapter 2

Politics, policy and disability

Man exists so that history shall exist, and history exists so that the truth can be revealed.

(Marx in Bottomore and Rubel 1963: 73)

INTRODUCTION

As we have already made clear, choosing where to begin is always arbitrary. Having chosen to start in the 1960s, we have to remember that the experiences of disabled people from this generation were shaped by decisions made and services provided in earlier decades. Most notably, we had the coming of the welfare state after the end of the Second World War and the infrastructure of services it established. While these services form the main backdrop for what follows, it also has to be remembered that the charity approaches to the problems of disability, which emerged in the nineteenth century, continued and indeed still continue to have an important influence.

THE LEGISLATIVE FRAMEWORK

The main pieces of legislation relevant to disabled people included the Disabled Persons (Employment) Act 1944, which was supposed to ensure reasonable access to paid employment for disabled people and which failed lamentably, largely because successive governments refused to enforce it. Then there was the Education Act (1944), which suggested that the most acceptable place to educate disabled children was in ordinary schools, but which in reality became the vehicle for establishing a massive range of segregated special schools whose power and influence remains largely unchallenged today. Next there was the National Health Services Act (1948), which, although establishing an impressive range of acute care hospitals, largely confined disabled people to geriatric wards. This was so at least until the 1960s, when a number of young chronic sick units were established, usually in the grounds of local hospitals. Finally there was the National Assistance Act (1948), which gave local authorities the power to provide either community-based or residential services for disabled people. In reality they provided few of the former and were often only too happy to purchase the latter from the old established charities or the newly emerging organisations, such as the Cheshire Foundation and the Spastics Society.

Despite the promises of the newly emerging welfare state for 'cradle-to-grave security for all', not all groups benefited to the extent that they might. The reality, by the 1960s, was that many disabled people were faced with the choice of managing with little or no service input or being shut away in a geriatric ward, a Cheshire Home or the like. Judy Hunt suggests that:

> What was happening was that there were two parallel groups of disabled people. There were those who lived in the community and nothing really began to happen. They were struggling with one set of issues and they were coping somehow in the community. Then there were those people who were in hospitals on chronic wards, geriatric wards and so on.

The existence of these two groups of disabled people provoked some debate about the kinds of service that should be provided. According to Hunt: 'there was a whole debate going on then about whether it was best for people to be cared for at separate places or whether they should stay in the community'. And she goes on to suggest that hospitals were inappropriate places for disabled people to live out their lives and that community services were more appropriate: 'they [policy makers] didn't really see how to make that a reality and at the end of the day it was thought that maybe different sorts of institutions or different sorts of places were needed to replace the hospital wards'.

EXPERIENCING SERVICES

The reality then, despite the infrastructure of services that had been established and the policy debates that had gone on, was that the majority of disabled people lived restricted lives, either in the community or in segregated establishments of one kind or another. Phillip Mason, who himself lived in residential accommodation for some time, suggests that we should not be too condemnatory of this:

> We have to try and think ourselves back into the late 1950s, which is very hard to do, otherwise we can't understand what the social norms were. They weren't particularly different in their attitudes and behaviour to other people in society. We were all much more accepting of authority, much more accepting of officialdom than we are today. It's impossible to imagine what it was like in those days but I can just remember being a schoolboy in the 1950s and nobody doubted authority – absolutely nobody. So we mustn't be too condemning of our brothers and sisters who lived in residential care at that time because that was the norm. Not just for disabled people in residential care but the norm for society.

Taking into account the period, we are not persuaded that such a generous and relativistic view can explain the conduct of the host of individuals who built successful careers on such practices. Some organisations, many still known to us today, grew, and remain, rich and powerful by removing disabled people from society. To understand our position, it is necessary to let disabled people describe some of their experiences in their own words. Joe Hennessey, for example, describes his experience of segregated special education:

> It was 300 miles away from home and I saw my parents only once a year, so it was pretty horrendous going away, having come from a loving family and with an extended family as well. That was pretty hairy to start with. But I suppose at that sort of age you get in and make relationships with other kids and it becomes less of a problem. It was a trauma going home every year for the summer holidays and coming back. I hated it. Not the going home; I loved the going home, I looked forward to it. But not the coming back; I hated it. But I was there supposedly for education. I never really knew why it was going to be a

problem for me to stay on at the local school. I think my parents,
with the education authority I imagine, were wanting me to get
some sort of treatment; to see if I could be made better and that
wasn't something that was possible in the north east so I came
down to London. From the age of 8 until I was 16 that's where I
was. Now, as I went through the teenage years, I suppose I
achieved a favoured position on the ward because I'd been
there a long time and I was older and maybe I was able to sort of
lead things. I was pretty much on the carpet in the matron's
office for doing all the sorts of things that you weren't supposed
to do. Being a little bit adventurous, not conforming to the very
tight rules of the school. So I was always being threatened with
expulsion.

Barbara Lisicki describes similar experiences and points to
significant differences between her and the staff:

It was a specialist hospital and kids and young people came
there from all over the country. I was there for 9 months with the
odd bit of weekend leave and went through an incredible
regime of awfulness and torture which they choose to call
physiotherapy and suchlike. The thing that struck me was that
there was a lot of working class kids there. But everybody that
ran it came from a more privileged background. I hadn't
actually had a huge amount of contact with people from that
kind of social background. But all the workers like the
physiotherapists, even people in what we would probably
regard as not very high status jobs like the ward clerk, were all
posh. I was a real sort of cockney sparrow and they made me
feel like dirt and I spent a lot of time feeling very angry that I
was treated in this way.

As well as links between special education and hospitals, there
were also close links between special schools and residential
homes. Nasa Begum describes her fears, and those of her peers,
about the possibilities of incarceration:

I remember at Treloars they introduced this education for life
course and certain people were taken to see the local Cheshire
Home and everyone knew, everyone knew what that meant.
Everyone knew what it meant if you were taken off in a bus.
Although we spoke about it, everyone dreaded your name
being up on the list.

Micheline Mason, whose experiences of special education led her to become one of the leading campaigners for inclusive education, describes her attempts to resist the system:

My 'special' boarding school was also fond of telling me that I had the wrong attitude, and that I was a troublemaker. My attempts to organise my friends at school to combat the oppressive attitudes of the staff were, of course, met with great resistance and hostility. I was split up from my comrades and put with other 'better behaved' young people on several occasions.

And she then details the outcome of such resistance:

Our self-esteem was so battered that most of us longed to be assimilated into the able-bodied world, believing this to be some kind of passport to eternal happiness. There is nothing like denying access to something to guarantee that you become obsessed with it.

Specialist colleges were often little better, and Ken Davis shows how his experience in one was linked to further segregated provision – the sheltered workshop:

It was a fairly harsh regime and a bit uncaring, insensitive to individuals and very much based on a competitive ethos. If you were good enough you would make it and if you couldn't make it through the college you weren't going to make it in the world of work anyway and you were probably destined for sheltered workshops. Indeed they ran a sheltered workshop as part of the college establishment in any event. But I got a job before I left that place, in Chesterfield, and that seemed to me to be the right thing to do. I was really just being able-bodied again in a way.

Where work was perceived not to be even a possibility, the employment service merely functioned to control disabled people in the community. Joe Hennessey graphically describes his experience trying to enter the labour market on leaving college and, in particular, shows how physical access problems to the specialist employment service were overcome:

I very much blamed them. I thought that excuses were being made. I wasn't getting this job and it didn't register truly with me then that there was a valid reason I didn't get the job. So I went on national assistance after I left the college, and claimed what was supplementary benefit at 15 bob a week. I couldn't get to the employment office to register because it was totally inaccessible. So we had an arrangement that I used to telephone from the one public phone box in the village. I used to telephone every week to the youth employment officer to register by phone. Then he would say whether there was anything in the pipeline – there never was.

Eventually he did get a job when he:

came under this disabled resettlement officer who had an upper limb impairment. So he understood a little bit about what it was like to be disabled. He got me a job at the local carpet factory as a carpet design stamper. It was producing punched cards for the carpet design. The carpet design was on very large sheets of graph paper where every little square represented a stitch in the carpet and I had to translate, line by line, onto this machine by putting in metal punches. And wherever the punch was, the hole came and so the hole on one line was supposed to be a yellow stitch in that position. If you got the holes punched wrong they got the wrong pattern on the carpet.

Community services prior to 1970 were provided through local welfare departments, which neither provided disabled people with the support systems necessary to live in the community nor saw much point in involving disabled people in discussions about what ought to be provided. According to Joe Hennessey:

In those days there were welfare departments run by the local medical officer of health. It was before Seebohm, it was before 1971. And we had tried to get representation on the local – I can't remember the correct title – but it was the welfare committee, if you like. So we wrote in to this great bureaucratic council and we had two lines in reply. 'You've been considered by the committee and your request has been declined.' Obviously they didn't want anybody on there who knew what it was all about and who would be arguing for changes or more resources, better services and God knows what else. That wouldn't help them.

The Health Service has often been called 'the jewel in the crown of the welfare state', and one of its most brightly shining facets would undoubtedly have been the National Spinal Injuries Centre at Stoke Mandeville Hospital. While its rehabilitation programme was geared towards 'independence', many disabled people on discharge were still faced with the difficult choice of managing in the community without support or going into residential care. The welfare ethos was that of 'living independently', not 'independent living'. If you could not manage without assistance then you were not independent but dependent – dependent on organised care that operated only within institutional environments.

Maggie Davis was faced with just such a dilemma:

> I was in an institution at Stoke Mandeville after my accident and I knew something was desperately wrong. I knew that I didn't have the rights that other people had; i.e. able-bodied people, but I couldn't figure out quite what it was all about. And I couldn't see why. I mean, being able-bodied before, I couldn't see why I just couldn't go back into society and have a flat and have somebody to help me and get a job. I actually presumed that this is what I would be able to do and I must admit I had a very rude awakening when there was nowhere to go, nobody would take me back in the job I had before, and there just wasn't any help in the community.

Stephen Bradshaw, who later became the first Director of the Spinal Injuries Association, was faced with a similar dilemma but resolved it differently:

> When I was first disabled I was very aware of the lack of state benefits. The way disabled people were treated back in 1968 when I came out of hospital was not good, and so I joined DIG [Disablement Income Group] straight away, because I thought that was the right way forward to gain basic and obvious things. Like benefits for women, for instance, which weren't available and it was very uphill all the way for disabled people. I got a noddy car so that's how I got about, and it was really through the fact that I was good at sport that actually I was able to socialise a lot. I was able to earn money carrying on my previous business so I didn't have to go out and find employment, so I was actually fortunate to be protected from a number of areas where, at that time, it was extremely difficult for disabled people to get jobs. If I hadn't had a family I could have gone back to, I would have been sent into an institution or whatever.

The only job proposal I had from Stoke Mandeville at the time, because I'd been in the printing trade, was why didn't I go up to Papworth and work in the department there that did printing. So it was very bad at that point.

FAMILY LIFE

While having a supportive family often kept people out of residential care, it did not always mean a fulfilled and unrestricted life. As Alice Etherington of People First told us:

Well in the earlier days I used to live with my parents. I wasn't allowed to do much even though I was over 18. I wasn't allowed to go out on my own, wasn't allowed to come back on my own, although I was allowed to go out with them if there were celebrations going on but that was a bit boring.

Even where some services supplemented family support, disabled people often still led restricted lives, as Ann MacFarlane describes:

I suppose it's useful to go back to the middle of the 1960s. It seems a long time ago but I think it's worth just saying that, for me, in the middle 60s I was living at home with my parents and my sister. I was working as a tutor. I had a three-wheel vehicle which I basically didn't want to drive because they never gave you any driving lessons – they just serviced and supplied the vehicles and the work that I did enabled me to be very self-contained. I was able to live within one to two rooms. I was able to concentrate purely on study and work and I certainly didn't have to meet hardly anybody. The few people that came in and out of the house, obviously I interacted with, but the only disabled people that I knew were those that I'd been in hospital with and one friend that I had met at a rehabilitation centre with whom I got on really well. We wrote to each other and she was near enough to visit once every two or three months, but she didn't regard herself as a disabled person. So really the issues around disability didn't arise in any deep or meaningful way.

Barbara Lisicki's father and brother had similar impairments, which gave her a certain self-confidence that other impaired people often do not have:

I wasn't a stranger to impairments because it has been born into my family, both my father and brother had impairments. Actually, my consciousness was from a very early age of really having to fight people's voyeurism and curiosity. Me and my other brother always used to pile in the noddy car with Andrew and we used to drive around. But when people used to stare at us when we went out together I used to say 'What do you think you are staring at?'. Even as a kid I was on one level challenging people's behaviour towards disabled people even though I wasn't a disabled person at that time.

Family life often brings tensions between the generations, which may be resolved when children move away from home. Where disabled children are involved this is often more difficult because of lack of available housing, and is often exacerbated as ageing parents find coping with the physical demands more difficult. Ann MacFarlane graphically illustrates this dilemma:

I think because I'd tried for a short while to get housing in the community and the options, the one or two bits of housing that were going to become available didn't materialise and I got really disheartened and I really thought I had to leave home. We'd had one or two difficulties around relationships and when my mother had broken her arm, that had shown me how woefully inadequate the existing services were. In fact, there weren't really any services at all so I couldn't get to work because there was no one to get me up in the mornings. That nearly cost me my job. It also showed me once a crisis occurs it could be long term.

THE MEDICAL MODEL RULES

Underpinning all this was what has come to be called the medical model of disability, which has had, and continues to have, a profound impact on the self-identity of many disabled people. Ann MacFarlane captures this process very well:

I think disability was very much illness-based for me. I was ill. I was perceived to be ill by everybody including the professional people and other people that visited me. I think I perceived myself as being ill, though in retrospect I certainly wasn't most of the time. I was ill at times but I wouldn't have said that was the predominant feature. The predominant feature throughout my institutional life was the fact that I was left in bed a lot of the time when I could have been up. Because I couldn't dress and wash myself, the staff did for me what they felt was adequate and sometimes it was totally inadequate. I was very much kept where they wanted me to be kept.

The medical model pervaded the consciousness of the other disabled people whom she was in contact with:

Certainly those people around me who had a disability didn't perceive themselves as in any way disabled. They focused and concentrated almost entirely on operations and it was the competitiveness that was sad. Those who perceived themselves to have the best surgeon, those who perceived themselves to have the most operations and those who perceived themselves to have the most serious illnesses thought they were the most important and the whole talk focused around those sorts of issues.

And, according to Phillip Mason, this medicalisation owes its origins to the development of the National Health Service:

That's where its roots were and many of the disabled people that came to Le Court came on the understanding that it was somewhere where they could make a life for themselves. Unfortunately, at about the same time or soon after, the National Health Service started and instead of being a place where they raised their own money and ran their own lives it rapidly became an institution, and a medical one at that. This was because of the National Health Service's imposition of the nursing criteria in the institution. And so people who had come to find and create a new life for themselves suddenly found themselves being imposed upon and having structures placed upon them which society really wanted because it was a nursing home and nursing homes have to be run along certain lines.

Despite the pervasive nature of the medical model, some people began to realise that all was not well and that resistance was necessary. Barbara Lisicki describes her own dawning consciousness:

I had begun to realise the oppressive nature of the medical

model but on a very individual level. At that time I did not know any better but they [the doctors] would want to do experimental operations and I let them. I just believed them. I didn't know to resist. I didn't know to say no. It didn't take me very long to learn – within four years I was saying to consultants 'Stuff your operations up your arse.' I didn't know it as a medical model. All I knew was that all these doctors were really screwing people. And they still are doing it. They are chopping bits of people off because they don't know how to deal with them.

Anne Rae, a long-time activist, makes the point that such resistance was usually individual; there were no disabled role models or organisations which could have given such actions a focus:

As a disabled person growing up at that time, there was nothing to identify yourself with. You couldn't identify with a group or anything like that; but I don't think I thought in those terms anyway. I think what we were desperately doing, what I was doing and probably all of us were doing, was normalising like mad, and reflecting what was going on around us. The 1960s was the era that people feel most nostalgic about these days. It was exciting, but those of us who were active and mobile in those days started to live in a pale reflection of how able-bodied society was organising at that time. Certainly disability consciousness or politics weren't on our agenda at that time.

VIEWS FROM ELSEWHERE

In trying to give an impressionistic picture of what life was like for disabled people in Britain in the 1960s, we have relied upon individual experience. To provide a more general picture we turn to Vic Finkelstein, who came to Britain having been expelled from South Africa. He later became a founder member of UPIAS and the first Chair of the BCODP, but here he describes his first impressions of Britain:

So when I came to Britain then I knew that there were a number of things happening although I didn't know the details – like there were DROs [disablement resettlement officers], the employment quota scheme and there were electric cars, and for me that was a lot. There were organisations like DIG. Early on then I was just completely confused. Then I met Liz [my wife] in Britain. She was a physiotherapist and had made a lot of contacts. She then introduced me to DIG and the ADP [Association of Disabled Professionals] was set up around then. Then I went along to a couple of these meetings. I was just terribly confused at that time.

Another immigrant from South Africa was Elsa Beckett, who has been involved in GEMMA for many years and who repre-sented that organisation on the Council of the BCODP when it was formed. She describes the collective disempowerment of disabled people in her early years in Britain:

Well, I only came to live permanently in Britain in 1969 so I was here for about ten years before the BCODP formed. Really I can't recall anything happening at all. I think we were just very disempowered. We're not that much better now but the whole kind of psychological feeling about disability was really back as it had always been. I don't think that we felt empowered to answer back, to even begin to talk about rights. That just wasn't there as far as I remember. It was supposed to be a great thing when services gradually came in so that you could get equip-ment. You could get some of your needs met, but the greater needs of the right to actual education, transport, employment and so on – that just wasn't mentioned as far as I remember. It just wasn't within our kind of scenario.

A SLOW, BURNING ANGER

Richard Wood, later to become Director of the BCODP, had a set of experiences, growing up with a disability in Britain, which fostered a slow, burning anger:

I've been through special school education. I've been through special college education and at the end of all that I've been rejected. At the end of being through the DRO system, of being sent away to do particular training and again I have been rejected. So it seemed that wherever the system was pointing me, it led nowhere. You spend time wondering whether it was there for them [those who worked in the services] more than it was there for you. That was a conclusion I reached long before I came to the movement. So I was burning with an anger that I still burn with but I didn't know how to express it and didn't know where I could express it. In Yorkshire, where I lived at the time, there was no movement. I didn't even know that there was a Derbyshire Coalition of Disabled People [DCDP].

This disempowerment fostered the same sort of anger in many other disabled people in Britain.

SMALL BEGINNINGS

There were already some organisations of disabled people in existence, with an honourable tradition of collective organising going back into the nineteenth century. Mike Barrett, long-time General Secretary of the National League of the Blind and Disabled (NLBD), reminds us of his organisation's impressive history:

We were linked with politics really from a very early age and within the first few years, within the first twenty years, we achieved things which have not been achieved since by disabled groups. The first thing that we did was we got infantile blindness recognised as a registrable disease with the help of the TUC [Trades Union Congress] and the Labour Party, and from that we saw the incidence drop from 36 per cent to 12 per cent after we got that piece of legislation into being. The second piece of legislation we saw come into operation was the Blind Persons' Act, 1920. This was the forerunner, in many respects, of making money available to assist disabled people. This was because local authorities and government then were able to make money available to sustain workshops and to provide workshops. So our aim was to campaign to get better conditions, wages and employment into the workshops during those early years, and we were also campaigning to get other benefits brought in. One of the things we achieved – by about 1938 – was that there used to be a pension which was allowable to people at the age of 50. Well we got it brought down to 40 for blind people – if they were out of employment they could draw a pension from 40 onwards. It wasn't a lot but it was there. The biggest problem was they let it slip when they did some alterations to the Act and nobody picked it up at that time, when the alterations came along. Also in 1936 we took up an allegiance with the Labour Party and we developed the Blind Persons' Charter with them. And that, in the end, established blind committees in every local authority throughout the country and we had a representative on every one of those blind committees.

For some disabled people, however, it was an oppressive personal experience that triggered a political consciousness and action. For Ann MacFarlane, it was attending the local craft class that was the trigger, although, as she goes on to explain, she did not get much support from other disabled people:

It was run by an occupational therapist and it was held in a room in a big Victorian house. It was basically a social couple of hours and these women used to come and make afternoon tea and pat us on the head and make us cakes. It was after I'd been going for some little while, probably 6 months or so, that discontent set in amongst us all because basically the place was dirty. We couldn't put our materials on the tables because they got messed up. It was cold and there was no carpet on the floor and there was a filthy path to walk up with holes that people used to fall into. After weeks and weeks of moaning I said 'Well, shouldn't we do something about it? Why shouldn't we have some luxury when we know that the doctor who sits in the office next door is knee deep in carpet?'. So they all said 'Oh, what a good idea, you can organise it and write the letter and we'll all agree.' So I wrote the letter and sent it and that was my first big mistake. Because I wrote it and I sent it, the next week I got called into see this doctor. He said 'What was the problem?' and I said, sitting there with my wheelchair on his carpet, 'Well you know you're sitting here in luxury and we haven't got anything and we all think that we should have some decent surroundings and some decent stuff – tables and things, and we need the path made up.' And he said he thought we were very ungrateful because we hadn't had anything before and now we've got this room and we had somewhere to come. And he came out of his room and he asked everybody what they thought because they were all sitting round this great big table. And they all said 'Oh no we're very happy here. We really like coming here. It's perfectly all right.' So when he left, of course, that was it. I said 'Well if that's how you tackle things then don't expect me to do anything on your behalf again.' So the next week I went back and then I left the week after that, even though everything was done. The path was made up. The tables were changed, the floors cleaned.

John Evans, who served on the Management Committee of the Spinal Injuries Association and became Chair of the BCODP, describes how going into a residential institution helped in that it overcame the sense of individual isolation many disabled people living in the community faced, and some still face today:

I was quite fortunate in a sense that I had problems after I became disabled about living in the community. I went to Le Court to live, which I didn't want to do, because I thought it was an institution and it had all sort of bad things that I didn't particularly think were the sorts of things that I wanted to be doing. But, as it happened, there were lots of things happening at Le Court and I immediately got in touch with disabled people being active. There was an active residents' committee, there was participation on the management committee, and disabled people were actually taking an active role in the running of the home and doing all sorts of things. So there was this kind of real positive feel to it even though it was a real institutional setting.

Phillip Mason, a one-time resident in the same institution, does not have quite the same view, and describes an incident which relates the politics of disability to political issues more generally:

I was a resident at Le Court and I did try, in my own perhaps more simple ways in those days, espousing some of the ideas that disabled people want to decide and choose for themselves. There was no flicker of recognition of what we were saying. One felt that there was no contact at all, no understanding. At one stage he [Leonard Cheshire] came and suggested that we all gave up our Christmas dinner and sent the money to a Cheshire home in India and he was astonished that we didn't even discuss it. He just thought that it was absolutely appalling. One can understand what he was trying to say but the fact that he felt able to come and make that proposal to the residents was the wrong spirit. It was virtually a dictate which the residents just wouldn't have contemplated. It was just a totally false proposal and it was based on some really very, very grossly misguided assumptions about disabled people. He assumed that we were just being selfish and ungrateful and exceedingly uncaring in refusing to discuss it. But in fact it was to do with lots of other issues as well. It wasn't to do with the state of people in India at all. It was to do with the fact that he should come along and make that suggestion. I've never held him in any high regard at all. I don't regard him at all as a war hero or anything. And I find this very hard to say this, this criticism, but I feel that he's been responsible for misleading society dreadfully. And I feel that very painfully because I am aware that during the formative years of the Foundation there was a very strong debate within the Foundation as to whether they should be building homes or whether they should be buying houses and letting them to disabled tenants. And I just think that the world of disabled people in this country would be so different if disabled people had been tenants. This was in the early days and if you imagine the amount of money that the foundation has recycled. It's millions and millions. And instead of building institutions, if they'd just gone into housing and enabled people to access housing it would have made a profound difference to the lives of disabled people. And the fact that this was a debate within the Foundation shows that even amongst able-bodied people there were people of vision who could see that what we have to do is help people stay where they are.

Nasa Begum, as we described earlier, visited Le Court from her special school but managed to stay out of its clutches. Instead she went into sheltered housing, which was not a happy experience:

Me and this other guy were both 'mega-hated' in this sheltered housing because we were seen as obnoxious, young radical disabled people. We were only radical because we didn't want to go to the church service and I didn't want to go to Yately Industries, which was an industrial workshop. But it was seen to be completely out of order.

By this time, some disabled people were becoming active in their local communities when issues relevant to disabled people were on the agenda. Joe Hennessey describes his initial experience thus:

The introduction of parking meters in Newcastle gave no consideration to the position of people with mobility problems and I remember going to this meeting and – I'm still what 20, 21, very young and having been from a rather sheltered hospital environment, not the big wider world. Me taking on these borough engineers and borough town planners and I can remember it now. I remember everybody in this huge room looking and fixing their eyes on me.

Often it was local branches of the Disabled Drivers' Association (DDA) who confronted such issues, although long-time member Anne Rae points to the limited political awareness which still existed among the membership:

> The DDA was essentially organised as a charity, and the charity ethic was welded into its consciousness. There was no consciousness at all that there were other disabled people outside of DDA who needed support, and that DDA should be campaigning for them.

CONCLUSIONS

The question this raises is how the disability movement emerged. In particular, given the picture we have painted of a massive infrastructure of complex, confusing and dependency-creating services and the existence of passive and disempowered disabled people, how did the movement become what it is today?

There were a few organisations of disabled people which had emerged out of working-class attempts at collective organisation, as Mike Barrett described, and others like the DDA, discussed by Joe Hennessey and Anne Rae. However, there was a whole plethora of other organisations which had developed out of the nineteenth-century charity ethic; according to one commentator: 'In the case of the disabled, until 1893 the only provision made was by voluntary charitable societies' (Topliss 1979: 13). Some of these, like the Royal National Institute for the Blind (RNIB) founded in 1868, had grown very large and rich by the 1960s.

There was a third group of organisations which had emerged in the first half of the twentieth century, largely from middle-class parents' groups, and which were becoming very powerful; MENCAP and the Spastics Society are the best examples of these. Finally, there was a fourth group of organisations which emerged after the Second World War and which David Hevey (1992) has called the single impairment charities; their main stated aim was to resource medical research to find a cure for the particular impairment.

None of these organisations is of concern to us here, for, as we have already indicated, they do not fit into our definition of the disability movement. They are relevant, however, in the sense that many disabled people became involved with such organisations in a variety of ways. Often, though, disabled people simply failed to join these organisations, or if they did join, they left in disillusionment, either because these organisations did not meet their personal or political needs or because they spent all of their energies on raising money for cures.

Thus, by the 1960s, as far as disabled people were concerned, we were faced with the choice of a range of dependency-creating services or nothing at all, and a plethora of disability organisations which spoke in our name but neither represented us accurately nor met our needs. It is scarcely surprising, therefore, that most of us were isolated, disempowered, impaired individuals. But, as we have already begun to describe, a political consciousness concerning disability issues was beginning to emerge among some disabled individuals. This is an issue that we will consider in much more detail in the following chapter.

Chapter 3

Disability organisations and the political process

The idea that expertise may grow as much from lived experience and reflection as from 'objective' academic study is still far from being universally accepted.

(Altman 1994: 128)

INTRODUCTION

The 1960s then were the decade when the new movement of disabled people began to emerge. However, we must emphasise that there were forerunners of this going back into the nineteenth century; organisations controlled by disabled people which had been modelled on working-class and trade union struggles. There was another kind of disability organisation beginning to emerge out of the charity ethic, so important in the nineteenth century. Some of these, despite changes of name, are still around today, but do not fall within our definition of the disability movement and so need not concern us further here.

Mike Barrett describes the emergence of his own organisation:

The first roots were laid in about 1893 and the reasons for this were that although many workshops had developed under voluntary organisations, it was becoming very obvious because they'd been running now for about 40 to 50 years that a lot of blind people were still not progressing. We were purely an organisation for blind people at that stage. We only had associate partially sighted members because it was meant for blind people; that is, people who were on the blind register. The main place for recruitment was within the blind workshops but it took six years to get some real substance into the movement so that we could start really thinking what kind of organisation we were going to be. Of course, we were industrially based and most of the work that blind people did was industrial. In 1866 there had been a Royal Commission on the Blind and the Deaf, and from that it was recommended that the government and local authorities should be giving financial assistance and other assistance to these groups of people. Nothing really came of that. By the time we got to 1899 we realised that with the explosion of the trade union movement and the industrial front as well, the most appropriate plan for us was to get into the trade union movement. Well we managed that and registered in 1899 as an independent trade union, and then we affiliated to the TUC in 1902. [Our ninetieth anniversary was] celebrated at the TUC congress ... We also realised that, because it was a strong labour movement, we needed to get politically involved and we affiliated to the Labour Party in 1909.

As we said in the last chapter, there was a range of other disability organisations around at this time, but they were not part of what we have defined as the disability movement simply because they were not democratic organisations accountable to disabled people. Anne Rae describes her experience with one of the larger organisations of this kind:

I got a job at the Spastics Society as the secretary to the then Sixty-Two Club organiser. The Sixty-Two Club was for people with cerebral palsy, and was very much a self-help thing. But, of course, it wasn't focused in quite that way. It was very much again an achieving thing; 'You can do it yourself', and you were exhorted to do so. It started to bother me that individual achievement was being emphasised, no matter what other problems people were struggling with. Nothing was going outwards to what we would now call disabling barriers; there was no concern with what was happening outside in the external world we were having to struggle with.

She goes on to suggest that the organisation, far from helping, was actually making matters worse:

What was happening within the Spastics Society itself was starting to come in and press down on me, because it was quite appalling; the lack of opportunity to discuss ideas of any kind. And I can remember a person I worked with one day came and said that as we were the only disabled people in the Spastics

Society, therefore we had to work that much harder and that much longer in order to prove to them that we were worth employing. I remember feeling absolutely enraged by that, and stating quite clearly that I'd been employed because I'd got the skills and qualifications to do the job, and that was the terms of my employment. I didn't feel I had any more to prove.

It could be said that the 1960s were the time when disabled people began to shake off the yoke of these organisations and organise things for themselves, partly because of the kinds of oppressive experience described above and partly because disabled people were beginning to feel that collective self-organising was the only way forward.

THE EMERGING MOVEMENT

Richard Wood locates the emerging movement in the history we have already discussed:

There have been organisations, particularly organisations of blind people, deaf people, who've been established for a long time. The NLBD have just had their hundredth anniversary. I think in many ways they were a focus. They were certainly a focus for disabled people, but they were a focus on a single issue and that issue was employment and everything that surrounded it. Their struggle was to establish a means of employment through sheltered working, because employers weren't taking the issue of disabled people in open employment on board.

Wood suggests that, as well as beginning to shake off the yoke of the old-established organisations, some disabled people were beginning to realise that the problems they faced went beyond access to employment:

I think what actually happened – going back into the 1960s now – was an awareness that the issues were far broader, the single issues that these single impairment groups had focused on weren't enough to satisfy the needs and aspirations of a wider range of disabled people. And I think what started to happen was that people began to realise that there was more to life than employment. And that, in fact, even thinking about employment required a lot of other things to be in place. And people began to realise that they weren't in place and started to say 'Well why aren't they in place? Why can't I use transport? Why can't I get in and out of this building? Or indeed more fundamentally, why can't I get out of bed?'. And so you have the growth of groups, not just in this country but also the States, that were a major influence on issues around the world. We had the embryo of organisations such as UPIAS, which possibly had a bigger impact on the growth and development of the move-ment in this country than the early CILs had on the growth of whatever the movement is in America.

It is certainly true that there was a new consciousness around disability issues emerging in the 1960s, and it is sometimes suggested that this emerged as a result of the influence of the civil rights and women's movement and of the IL movement in the USA. While these movements may have influenced the tactics and the direction of the disability movement in Britain, as John Evans makes clear, our movement was rooted in its own historical and material conditions:

So there was I think a bit of a conflict there really of interest and intention and also the pride of being British, of wanting to do our own thing in our own way without these imperialistic Americans telling us what to do. But I think in the end what happened was our own version anyway.

JOINING AN ORGANISATION

For many disabled people, local disability organisations or local branches of national organisations were the first point of contact. Joe Hennessey joined one such group 'purely for social reasons':

I'd come back to this local community after eight years of being away. The people I'd originally gone to school with were grown up like me but I hadn't shared my school days with them. I'd been there for a couple of years. They were all doing their own things and were now doing apprenticeships and so on. But I had no peer group. So I had heard about the DDA as it then was, a tricycle association. There was a local branch a few miles away.

Alan Pinn had a similar experience and describes how this developed into something more political:

I suppose it was about 1962 when I joined the local committee of the DDA. The local branch was the Twickenham District Group, I think it was called then. And it was there for the first time that I met a number of other disabled people and saw that perhaps there was a bit more that I could do, and I got involved right from very early days meeting other disabled people. I got involved in social events – a lot of them based round using our tricycles to meet, go on outings and so on. I didn't get heavily involved at that stage in any sort of campaigning issues. It wasn't till two or three years later that I started getting involved in any campaigning issues, and then it was particularly to do with mobility and the tricycle and driving. I was still able to drive at that stage. I remember writing my first letter to the editor of the local paper when I was still quite young, about 20 I think. It was concerning the introduction in Kingston of parking meters and the fact that there were going to be no concessions at all for disabled people. I just wrote a letter to the paper saying that I felt it was a mistake that disabled people weren't being considered. With the backing of our organisation and some other noises made by other people, eventually concessions were given. I suppose that was my very first sort of involvement in any campaign, and then it progressed from there.

Coming together and beginning to organise around particular issues had a consciousness-raising effect which forced disabled people to consider some of the wider issues. Joe Hennessey explains:

It was the coming together and realising from other people the common problems that they had and that very few of them were in employment. Most of them were on low incomes. I could see that there was a status, a very inferior status to being disabled. So that's when I began to become aware of major issues like access, because you had to be very careful about where you went. You couldn't get into public loos.

It was from such a base that he branched out and came into contact with some of the local charitable organisations for the disabled:

Being part of the ITA [Invalid Tricycle Association] was crucial to that and to the other things that I then branched out in. The local co-ordinating body for disabled people had the dowager duchesses – large ladies in floppy hats and floppy bosoms, county set – running the organisation.

Millie Hill, on coming to Britain from Canada, encountered a similar 'county'-type organisation right in the middle of London:

Hammersmith and Fulham Action for Disability has been in existence for about seventeen years and up until about five years ago it was run very much on the old lines, the paternalistic lines. The organisation was led primarily by non-disabled retired gentlemen who really felt that they were doing good work by helping these poor disabled people. And as a consequence of that type of attitude and that approach to so called bettering the lives of disabled people, they hired in primarily non-disabled staff who just perpetuated that old-fashioned idea that disabled people were there to be looked after and cared for and that they couldn't take decisions for themselves. It began to change, I think, if I can remember correctly, because of outside influences – other organisations of disabled people were saying that organisations which are in existence to promote the welfare of disabled people should actually be managed and controlled by disabled people themselves.

Rachel Hurst, past Chair of the BCODP and now their representative on the European Regional Council of DPI, had a similar experience with her own local association. Like Millie Hill, she suggests external influences shaped the transition of the organisation from one 'for' to one 'of' disabled people:

I joined GAD [Greenwich Association of Disabled People], which, although it had been called an organisation of disabled people since its inception in 1975, it certainly was not by any stretch of the imagination. In fact by the time I actually joined them officially, in 1978 or 1979, there were three of us who were tokens. My first introduction to the movement was through the television programme about the Berkeley CIL. That was in 1980 and it was like heaven, absolute heaven. And I immediately got in touch with them.

Such organisations provided both emotional and practical support which was of immense value to many disabled people. The emotional dimension is captured by Elsa Beckett: 'The fact was that there they were, disabled people together unashamedly and unselfconsciously talking about disability, talking about their experience.' Maggie Davis describes the practical value of such contacts 'through the usual process of mutual self-help':

> Somebody said, 'There's a disabled woman down the road, she'd been desperate to get driving, do you think you could take your car round and show her?'. I said, 'Yeah, no problem', and I took my car round. She ended up getting a Mini and getting on the road. So we had a friendship.

Not all disabled individuals found contact with other disabled people empowering. Sian Vasey describes her experience thus:

> I was just terribly well placed and I had already met the UPIAS when I was at school. Briefly, Paul Hunt and Vic Finkelstein had been down to Treloars one weekend and they'd done a presentation and it went down like a cup of cold sick, quite honestly.

And Micheline Mason describes a painful encounter:

> At this time [1976–8] there was no organised disability movement in the UK. I believe UPIAS existed, and I was pleased to know that, but having been emotionally and intellectually battered to the floor by one of its leaders, it did not feel it was like anything to which I wanted to belong.

THE EMERGENCE OF ORGANISATIONS OF DISABLED PEOPLE

A crucial factor in the emergence of the disability movement was the fact that disabled people were not sharing the wealth of the affluent society that was emerging in the 1960s. By this time, Britain had emerged from the poverty of the war and, with the economy booming, Harold Macmillan's phrase 'You've never had it so good' captured the spirit of the time. For many disabled people, it remained as bad as it always had been.

The idea of a national disability income emerged and was promoted as the way to ensure that disabled people were able to share in the affluence of the time. Colin Low describes the emergence of a number of organisations whose main goal was to achieve it:

The DIG was responsible for a great deal of policy development in the disability income field. Although not strictly an organisation of disabled people, it had notable disabled leaders in the persons of Megan Duboisson, Mary Greaves and Peter Large. [Peter Large and colleagues were also responsible for the foundation of the ADP in 1971.] Similar points could also be made about the Disability Alliance [DA], a broadly based coalition of organisations which came together in pursuit of the single goal of a comprehensive disability income in 1974. This too was not an organisation of disabled people – it was not a unitary organisation at all – but had significant input from disabled people, such as Fred Reid and myself, from the start.

Ken Davis, who later became a member of UPIAS, joined DIG and noted its connections with the Fabian socialist tradition:

I had joined DIG some years earlier because I recognised that [income] was important. It happened that, at about the same time, I got interested in Fabian literature, which probably came through reading DIG's magazine, which was called *Progress* in those days.

Rosalie Wilkins, who was later very influential in developing the *LINK* television programme, joined in a roundabout way:

My sister got involved with DIG first. She wanted to find out how to get the loos adapted at the Newport Pagnell Service Station. She then went on the early marches. She got involved on my behalf but it became important to me after I left university.

For her, it was not the income issue which was important, for: 'DIG was the coming together of all impairments. It wasn't just the income issue which I couldn't get my head around but it was more the coming together and sharing ideas.'

Vic Finkelstein also joined DIG, but it was a meeting with Paul Hunt, whom many of us regard as the founder of the modern movement, which raised crucial questions for him about the direction of the movement:

Around about that time I met Paul Hunt at an ADP meeting and we started discussing things, and he then started raising things which were in many ways foreign to me. But what was striking for me was that the criticisms that he was raising were very similar to the criticisms black people raise in South Africa. That was the connection for me. Otherwise I probably would have carried on for a long while. I guess I would have become disillusioned with DIG and ADP as well and I would have started getting more and more critical. I thought ADP had a limited perspective on many issues, but I always thought it was very clear on the issue that employment should be more accessible to disabled people. So disabled professionals set up their organisation on a class basis – the only class-based disability organisation that I know!

It was out of this meeting and subsequent discussions that UPIAS emerged:

I started attending various meetings and set a meeting up with Paul Hunt, who lived in Cheshire Homes at the time. I knew about the Cheshire Homes but Paul introduced me to the real criticisms about them, about the institution approach. It seemed to me that the clearest perception of what was wrong with disability was in relation to these homes. It was around the issue of controlling your life and the ability to get out of the homes and to get into the community, which then raised the income issue. We had a lot of discussions on that and Paul's position was that the DIG focus was not addressing those kinds of issues at all. The position that UPIAS then took was that if you understood what was happening with the homes you actually understood a lot about disability. Basically it goes back – and I'm using the words that I have now – to the fact that disabled people are socially dead so you don't need a home. We didn't use those terms but that's what it was about. As long as special homes existed for disabled people, even if you lived in the community, it was always a threat to you. There was always the possibility that you would be forced into one. We needed to address that issue and he felt that the various proposals coming out from DIG were not addressing the major issue. I didn't know the ins and outs of the argument but, looking back, the thing that really struck me, and which Paul was absolutely clear about, was that disabled people were not particularly involved and were easily excluded from the debates. It was the debates about economics which required specialist skills that Paul was concerned with. For him, disabled people themselves must control their lives, and while you've got the institutions they were denied control. That, for him, was the key issue.

By the 1970s there was major tension in the emerging movement between what might be called the incomes and the oppression approaches to disability. The DA was formed to take forward the former, and UPIAS became a think-tank to develop the latter. Paddy Ladd describes his experiences with both organisations:

> My experience begins from when we set up the National Union of the Deaf [NUD] in 1976. Our concern was to become a deaf-led pressure group in the UK and our major concerns were deaf issues. We were greatly encouraged and aided by the NLBD, as they took a union/socialist approach, but got no response from the NFB [National Federation of the Blind]. After reading UPIAS literature, we arranged a meeting with them, but they proved completely intransigent on the issue of deaf schools, which is and was a cornerstone of the deaf culture and history. We thus had nothing more to do with them. The contrast with the NLBD was only too clear; the latter, like us, saw no shame in organising at grassroots level, or in celebrating the everyday lives of the people in those places. These issues, among others, continue to divide the deaf/disabled movements to this day and will continue to do so until we are listened to by disabled people.
>
> We then turned to the DA, in fact we were recruited by them to assist with their deaf booklet. Despite criticisms of the DA they did offer us respect for our views, and their policy did offer a way out from the charity dependency philosophy. In working with their members, we were able to access political ideas and people with influence, which was of great importance to a fledgling NUD, particularly as we were under heavy fire from organisations *for* the deaf.

COLLECTIVE MOVEMENTS NEED INDIVIDUALS

No account of the origins of the emerging movement would be complete without mention of some of the individuals involved. There is a considerable literature on why individuals join movements, but we do not intend to deal with any of the psychological explanations (conflict over authority, substitute communities or aggression/frustration hypotheses), as these seem wholly inadequate.

Most of the people we interviewed, or others we have met in the movement, joined because they gradually came to realise that the problems they faced were not theirs alone and that the only solution, in the end, was to organise with others facing similar difficulties. As well as a desire to improve the conditions of their own lives, there was often a desire to improve those of other disabled people as well. In referring to individuals, there is always a danger, of course, that key people will be missed out. What we are keen to provide, however, is a view of some of the individuals who were developing the two approaches of the emerging movement: the incomes and oppression approaches.

Stephen Bradshaw mentions meetings with key individuals from both approaches:

I met Peter Large very early on, and it was because disabled people were involved in DIG that I saw the pressure for change coming from disabled people with a number of able-bodied people helping them, rather than the RADAR [Royal Association for Disability and Rehabilitation] approach, which had lots of able-bodied people who were involved and only one or two disabled people – rather the other way round. I didn't make any sort of connection in terms of 'of' and 'for' organisations at that time.

I discussed things with Vic [Finkelstein] quite a bit. SIA [Spinal Injuries Association] came up and you know I was there at the Steering Committee, but I was involved in my own business and so I didn't intend to get closely involved or employed by SIA. Obviously I supported it, because I saw very clearly that the spinal units weren't the only answer, and the answer was that disabled people had to get organised to protect their interests and actually spread their own knowledge.

Phillip Mason suggests that the oppression approach can be traced back to:

Paul Hunt, of course, who knew that the future lay in raising the awareness and political aspirations of disabled people in the community, and he, outside of any established organisation, started UPIAS. It was Paul Hunt's tradition. It was the tradition of the residents. We regard that as our inheritance. It was perhaps the greatest gift that we could have been given.

Peter Wade, who had been a long-time colleague of Paul Hunt's and also lived in Le Court, had a different idea about how to change things. As Phillip Mason explains: 'The tragedy is that Peter thought that the future lay in working within established systems to change them and so he joined RADAR and the Cheshire Foundation.' However, as Mason relates, this decision was not a happy one:

In 1979 we started Project 81, which was a group of disabled people trying to leave Le Court. He joined us and gradually over the time he became more and more involved. He got more and more excited and within a year of his death he'd resigned from RADAR and resigned from the Cheshire Foundation and very tearfully admitted that he hadn't achieved what he thought he could achieve. He was a very, very sad man. And I felt desperately sorry for him because I was very fond of Peter and he was a genuine worker. He was a genuine man of our cause, but he thought the future lay in reforming these groups and he hadn't succeeded and he admitted it.

Peter Wade's experience was, and still is, a very common one for those who strive to change traditional 'caring' organisations from within, and is a major reason why the BCODP adopted a policy of organising quite separately from such bodies. It was not until 1991, under a benefits consortium, that the BCODP felt strong enough to collaborate in a joint initiative with the large organisations for disabled people. Even at the time of writing in 1995, when organisations 'for' and 'of' have joined a common consortium to campaign for civil rights legislation under the banner of the Rights Now Campaign, there remain great tensions between the two juxtaposed positions and approaches. What is so different now is that the disability movement has been calling the shots with increasing confidence and power, going into places they refused to go only three years ago.

Not everyone came to the same conclusion as Peter Wade, and again, Colin Low provides an articulate defence of working with traditional organisations:

But within my knowledge, it was the NFB which did more than any other organisation from the outset, but particularly in the

1970s, to work out a comprehensive set of policies designed to underpin the emancipation, integration and advancement of blind and disabled people in society. People like Ken Whitton, Martin Milligan, Fred Reid and I were deeply involved in working out detailed policies covering the complete range of public and service areas – integration in education, participation in organisations providing services for the blind, employment, financial compensation, social services, access and the environment. We wrote numerous submissions based on these policies and, as well as submitting them to government, fed them in through official and semi-official committees on which we managed to gain places, such as Lord Snowdon's Working Party on the Integration of the Disabled, the Silver Jubilee Committee on Access for the Disabled, and the Committee on Restrictions against Disabled People. Perhaps of interest is the fact that I made minority recommendations in favour of anti-discrimination legislation [ADL] to the first of these bodies and made sure that the issue was raised again by the second. This led to the setting up of the third, with an express remit to investigate the question of ADL, and I took a leading hand in seeing that it came out with a strong recommendation in favour. These three committees operated over a two-year time span each between 1974 and 1981.

BUILDING ALLIANCES

Many disabled people began to recognise that self-organisation was not enough, and that it was necessary to involve others. As Joe Hennessey says:

> We wanted to form a local co-ordinating body. I suppose a pressure group was what we were really after. We wanted to be able to come together and get things done. Yes disabled people themselves, but we'd also invited other local organisations as well as the local authorities and the health service to come together, so that we could say 'We want to work, we want recognition, we want to be able to have a meaningful dialogue and we want things doing.'

However, the response was perhaps not as welcoming as it might have been:

The idea was firmly sat on by all the people from the statutory bodies and from the county association for 'the disabled'. So all that happened after that was that we carried on doing our own local pressure group activities and linking up with other DDA branches in the area.

Some authorities had their own ideas about what consulting disabled people actually meant. Phillip Mason describes the situation in the area where he lived:

We had in Hampshire, during the 70s, one person who was regarded as being the voice of disabled people in Hampshire. No accountability. No constituency. No reference to a constituency. In fact this person was the 'crip mouth'. He spoke for disabled people. And I think that's what happened in the past, with people like Douglas Bader and others like that.

But in the 1970s it was building alliances with or being influenced by other groups of disabled people that was crucial, not trying to develop alliances with the statutory sector or the local voluntary organisations. According to John Evans:

It was quite an exciting time. Phillip Mason and myself got together and threw around some ideas, and we said 'Right, we've got to do something about this', and we formed Project 81. Even though there was no disability movement around then you really felt you were part of something. Once we got onto finding out how to go about things, we suddenly met Ken and Maggie Davis up in Derby and the Grove Road Scheme that they got involved in, and Steve Burton in London setting up SHAD [Specialist Housing Association for Disabled People], and there seemed to be all these different things going on that we hadn't known about. To a certain extent to me it was like there was this disability movement. There were disabled people actually doing similar things in different parts of the country to what we were trying to do in Hampshire. I suppose everyone was doing it in different ways really.

Again, John Evans stresses the importance in learning from other disabled people, and not just in Britain:

We wrote to the States and we got information from Berkeley and from a number of other CILs, and that definitely had an influence on us, without a doubt. There were also a number of

TV programmes coming along about it, so all of a sudden we were invaded in the early 80s by all this information coming through. That definitely had an effect, and I went out to the States in 1981 beginning to do a research project. I visited four different CILs and so I had first-hand experience of what was going on there. It definitely did have an influence, without a doubt, even though we realised the systems in the States and in this country were different.

CONCLUSIONS

Researchers who have studied social movements provide four kinds of theory as to their emergence: strain theories, mass society theories, resource mobilisation theories and political process theories (Marx and McAdam 1994). Strain theories suggest that some kind of problem or conflict exists and 'collective action arises out of people's efforts to cope with the stresses of life in a social system under strain' (Marx and McAdam 1994: 78). Mass society theories suggest that in times of rapid social change some groups are excluded or disenfranchised and collective behaviour emerges as a response. Resource mobilisation theories suggest that collective behaviour emerges only under particular economic and social conditions; that is, sufficient wealth to support such activity. Political process theories suggest that movements emerge as a reaction to unresponsive existing political institutions and processes.

These theories are not intended to be mutually exclusive, and they can all be applied to the emergence of the disability movement. There was clearly strain in society in the 1960s in that disabled people were not getting a fair share, or even any share, in the affluence that was emerging. It was also a time of rapid social change and, as well as being affluent, the 1960s were swinging as well. Disabled people, however, began organising collectively in order to secure a reasonable standard of life, not because they wanted to participate in rapid social change.

It is also clear that the increasing affluence of the 1960s did raise the expectations of disabled people, but this only served to highlight the inadequacies of the existing political institutions to provide disabled people with the necessary resources to lead a reasonable life. It further demonstrated, to disabled people at least, that the existing disability organisations could not be relied upon to articulate the views of disabled people.

So while these theories may help to explain why the movement emerged, they do not explain why it emerged when it did. To do that we need to return to what John Evans called 'our own version'. There are two aspects to this. First, Britain in the 1960s had recovered from the effects of the war and was entering an age of affluence, when people were told and believed that they had never had it so good. Except, of course, disabled people, who in the main remained poor and excluded from society, whether they lived in their own homes or institutions.

The second specific aspect of our own version was the existence of a significant number of residential institutions established after 1948, in which a large number of disabled people were not only incarcerated but slowly coming to realise the injustice of such incarceration. These factors gave rise to the emergence of DIG and UPIAS, both of which are crucial to the development of the movement.

These then are the two specific reasons why the movement emerged at the time that it did, with DIG and UPIAS being the foundation stones on which it was based. In the next chapter we will consider how these foundation stones were built upon.

Chapter 4

The rise of the disability movement

> It is difficult for isolated individuals to engage in effective political action; political participation is facilitated by the existence of social networks or political organisations that coordinate the actions of many individuals.
>
> (Inglehart 1990: 43)

INTRODUCTION

The gradual recognition by disabled people that neither party politics nor charitable and voluntary organisations were serving their interests appropriately or well is a key factor in the emergence of the movement. There were also a number of external influences such as the civil rights movement and feminism, both of which had succeeded in getting the outlawing of discrimination on the grounds of race and gender onto the statute books in Britain. This in turn influenced the emerging consciousness of disabled people, who were beginning to recognise that the problem of disability is externally located and that our exclusion from society is a human rights issue.

As we have described in the previous chapter, the conditions for the emergence of something new or different had been created as far as disability organisations were concerned. Maggie and Ken Davis describe these conditions perfectly:

> It was about the need for a mass movement among disabled people, for disabled people to be mobilised. The argument basically was this – whilst there might have been a time in history when it was perfectly reasonable for disabled people to have been segregated and incarcerated, the growth of technology and the availability of wealth in British society had reached

the point where there was no longer any justification for disabled people to be left on the side lines. There was no longer any need for disabled people to be segregated because the technological wealth and other means existed to change all that. What was needed to change all that was a mass movement among disabled people, controlled by disabled people themselves. Within this, the role of able-bodied people, experts, professionals and anybody else, would be to support disabled people to articulate and to take the lead in their own emancipation.

FALSE STARTS ON THE ROAD TO LIBERATION

The incomes approach to the problems of disabled people had held out much promise in the late 1960s and early 1970s and, buttressed by the passage of the Chronically Sick and Disabled Persons Act (1970), a new day appeared to be dawning for disabled people. However, both the incomes approach and the new legislation promised more than they ever delivered, and by the late 1970s, they appeared to be a false start to many disabled people.

The problem for DIG was that a schism quickly developed between those who wanted to become a single-issue lobbying group and those who wanted to become a mass movement. Rosalie Wilkins was involved and describes what happened: 'Quite soon the issue around the division between the grass roots and those walking the corridors of power emerged. There were some fascinating battles around that. In the end it became very divisive.' Ken and Maggie relate the failure of DIG to its development as an 'expert' rather than a 'mass' organisation:

> Well basically DIG's lack of success in establishing a national disability income was due to it, broadly speaking, falling into the hands of the experts – many of whom were able-bodied – who were good at arguing and lobbying Parliament, and because it had become remote from grassroots membership. The membership was little more than fundraising fodder for this elite group of well-versed parliamentary lobbyists. That was perceived as being quite the wrong direction if disabled people were going to get a national disability income.

It would have signalled a return to the professionals speaking on behalf of disabled people rather than democratically representing a mass directive from them.

UPIAS, on the other hand, was committed to a very different approach. Vic Finkelstein spells this out:

> Disability wasn't about being under the control of others, particularly medical control – it's all in the Policy Document [UPIAS 1976]. It was about disabled people controlling their own lives with the support they needed. The document also asserted that disability should not be looked at in small bits; it needed to be looked at as a totality. Again that was a direct criticism of DIG. I think that was the thing that arose mainly from my discussions with Paul [Hunt]. The failure of DIG was due to its failure to see disability broadly. Although I gather from the original dissension at DIG that its aims were broader, but they got narrowed down very quickly. It was a broader perspective that turned into a benefits approach. The two principles that Paul really clarified were disabled people's control over their own lives and that disability is not a single issue.

Rosalie Wilkins, however, having seen what had happened to DIG, none the less felt unable to join UPIAS because of its unyielding commitment to these principles: 'I found it was difficult to join the Union. I was attracted to the ideas but I couldn't be that whole-hearted.'

DEMOCRACY HAS BEEN COMING: SMALL BEGINNINGS

Phillip Mason pays tribute to the intellectual work of Paul Hunt while he was in Le Court: 'Paul Hunt was the thinker. He actually clarified the issues and what they revolved around and enabled residents to know what to fight for.' There is no doubt in our minds that Paul Hunt was pivotal to the emergence of the disability movement as we have defined it; that is, the movement that emerged in the 1970s. Not only had he produced the first important book written by disabled people about disability issues (Hunt 1966) but he was able to inspire others. Paul had three essential ingredients that make for a natural leader. First, he clearly communicated the new ideas to a variety of audiences by writing in the popular press, specialist journals and disability newsletters, as well as individual letters of encouragement to disabled people seeking his advice and guidance. Second, he practically organised disabled people to take control of their situations (Le Court residents' strikes and management takeover were the first examples of direct action instigated by Paul). Third, in collaboration with others, Paul set in motion the formation of UPIAS, which set up the infrastructure and fundamental principles for future political representation.

Just as DIG had started with a letter in the *Guardian*, so some years later did UPIAS. As Ken Davis reminds us:

> Paul Hunt had written a letter saying that basically the time had come for disabled people to consider taking up the cudgels on their own behalf. I can't remember the exact wording, but he invited people to write to him and we did.

The letter was instrumental in the formation of UPIAS; many responded to Paul's invitation to write to him:

> Severely physically handicapped people find themselves in isolated, unsuitable institutions, where their views are ignored and they are subject to authoritarian and often cruel regimes.
>
> I am proposing the formulation of a consumer group to put forward nationally the views of actual and potential residents of these successors to the workhouse.
>
> (*Guardian*, 20 September 1972)

Anne Rae saw the letter and responded. She soon joined the organisation and, while living in the community herself, she began to visit disabled people in institutions:

> I'd seen a short letter in the *Guardian* by Paul Hunt about a different approach to issues around being disabled. I'd written to them and said I'd be interested in talking to them, and joined UPIAS in that way. I got some of their literature and started to correspond with them. And actually I started to visit institutions to talk about what people felt about being in an institution, whether they felt there was something else that they could have done or would like to do.

The new organisation, according to Ken and Maggie, very quickly set about developing its own modus operandi:

> It led to the formation of what later became known as the Union

for the Physically Impaired Against Segregation. Vic Finkelstein was an early respondent and member. We met in London
and corresponded regularly, but the main vehicle for discussions for people who had responded was an internal circular,
which was agreed to be confidential to the members. This was
because so many people were in institutional care. It was very
important that they could feel secure about being able to share
their thoughts and experiences and speak freely without fear of
retribution. So that was the agreement. It remained a confidential internal circular for many years after that. The important set
of circulars was of those in the lead-up to the formulation of the
policy statement and the constitution.

And just as there were subsequent debates about the name of the
BCODP, so too were there about UPIAS. Ken and Maggie illustrate
that there were more than simply semantic issues at stake:

Some people wanted to call it the Union of the Physically
Impaired for Integration. That in itself was a major debate. The
debate was something like this: 'Well I think it's positive to
think of where you want to go and all of that.' Then the other
side of that was – 'Well you've only got to look at what actually
happens in practice. There are thousands of people for integration and at the same time as they are saying it, they're practising
segregation.' It's politically harder for people to say they're
against segregation and continue working in a segregative way.

As well as being committed to fundamental principles, UPIAS
also quickly became an organisation with very strong internal
discipline, as Ken and Maggie make clear:

It was open to any disabled person but the weeding-out process
was an internal one. A number of members went on to become
members of the Liberation Network [LNDP], which was a
much more liberal, literally loose network. The Union, at the
time, was very committed to the political requirement facing
disabled people, which was to produce a rigorous, dependable
explanation of disability in social terms that enabled society
itself to be seen as the focal point of disabled people's attention.
That very fact required disabled people to actually organise if
they were to be effective and do anything about it. Loose
networks of liberal-minded, well-meaning disabled people

were not actually going to produce the cutting edge that was necessary to start a mass movement.

For some, UPIAS quickly developed a reputation for being secretive and exclusionary. In this sense it grappled with an issue that many other social movements have faced; whether and whom to exclude from joining. Vic Finkelstein explains the rationale for this:

> Before you can develop a clear understanding of disability, the group most concerned needs to address it and look at it and understand it. When it's done that, then others can come in. But if you bring others in before you've done that, then because the group is an oppressed group, it will have less experience and less capabilities than the other people who have come in, and they will modify it on their terms. So if you have able-bodied people included with the experiences they will bring, their perception will modify the group. So you've got to exclude other groups. That was the key thing. Setting up the Union so it was only open to disabled people was point one. The second point was that it was targeted at people in institutions. We very quickly became aware, because Paul and the others knew already, that people in institutions are vulnerable. Any criticisms about the institutions and they were liable to be treated badly. So that is why we made it confidential; that's the reason for it. So the membership was restricted to these two things. One, it was restricted to disabled people, and two, it was a confidential thing. People thought it was secretive but that was the reason for it.

There were other criticisms that were levelled at UPIAS, and similarly have been used to attack the BCODP; namely that it was male-dominated and male-oriented. Maggie Davis provides an internal critique of this:

> Well it can be criticised from all kinds of points of view. From the female perspective I'm sure that there was more than a hint of a hard, not necessarily macho, style in terms of the political and analytical debate; in terms of the dialectic and the rigour by which people were expected to defend their positions and stand or fall by them in a process of self, personal development within the collective ethos. In some senses that has got a very typical masculine political feel to it and I think that it [UPIAS]

has to live with that kind of criticism. Later on, when we [the women involved] looked back at the circulars, we saw that fairly clearly. Although we still agreed that it was the right direction that we took.

But the collective experience of the group was also a very supportive one, as Ken Davis explains:

The other side of the Union was very different; the side that people didn't see, because when they looked at what they heard about the Union or what the Union had written publicly they saw the sharp intellectual cutting edge, if you like. But behind that there were the most enormous personal, intensely supportive relationships going on all the way down the line, with members nearly killing themselves to support each other and to be active in the debates.

Thus, according to Ken Davis, the work done by UPIAS became the intellectual heart of the newly emerging disability movement:

Personally I think when you look at the movement overall, if there wasn't a theoretical heart to the movement, the movement would free float. If there wasn't discipline the movement would equally free float. One of the major contributions made by the Union, if not the major contribution, was that it did provide the intellectual heart and the political heart of the movement.

While there was some ambiguity over whether UPIAS itself would become a mass movement, or merely the vanguard out of which a mass movement would emerge, it is true that it never built up a large membership. According to Vic Finkelstein:

It was always intended that UPIAS would have a non-sectarian approach, but people weren't joining. We had a lot of discussion about why people weren't joining and whether we should become more populist or not. There really was a problem in the disabled community. It wasn't so much a problem with the Union as such, although there were problems with the Union. The main problem was that disabled people in their isolation were ignorant about disability issues.

Two of the possible reasons for this have already been alluded to; its male dominance and its internal discipline.

Micheline Mason wanted a different kind of organisation:

'What I wanted, and initiated, was a coming together of "leaders" of different fragments of disabled people's struggles, to have a "safe haven" in which to think, plan and strategise collectively.' Accordingly, Micheline's view of the LNDP was different from that of Ken and Maggie Davis, referred to earlier:

> LNDP was a woman-led organisation and it embodied female values, although it included men right from the beginning. Through the support groups, and later through the magazine *In from the Cold*, we began to challenge the traditional view of disability as an individual health problem. We challenged the effects of 'internalised oppression', recognised by all marginalised groups as the major 'tool' of the oppressive society; we challenged the conditioned hatred of ourselves and each other as disabled people; we challenged the desire to assimilate; we challenged the denial of 'hidden' disabilities; we challenged the fierce competition between us; we challenged the inability to champion, appreciate and support each other's achievements or thinking (especially when it challenges our own); we challenged the lack of information and understanding about the issues of other oppressed peoples.

This was clearly an impressive and extensive agenda for any organisation to deliver, and the Network was unable to carry it through. Micheline explains:

> Unfortunately, being women-led, it was prey to sexism. Firstly, in the dismissal of its achievements and theoretical basis, and secondly, in the fact that the women leading became subsumed by traditional female roles of child-care, husband care and cleaning up messes.

Despite this and its demise by the middle of the 1980s, according to Micheline, and borrowing from the words of the leader of another very different political movement, it enabled 'a thousand flowers to bloom'. It was, therefore, critical in providing a less intensive forum for activists to debate ideas:

> It is impossible to quantify or judge the effect of the Network on the disability movement. I believe it sowed many seeds which have come to flower. All the people involved are still leading and developing in different areas, and most speak of the Network days with great nostalgia.

SINGLE-IMPAIRMENT BUT DEMOCRATIC

There was another kind of organisation to emerge in the 1970s; single-impairment groups, of which SIA became the largest and most important. It was different from the earlier single-impairment groups, whose main activities centred on fund raising to find a cure. Instead it emerged as a democratic and accountable self-help group whose control was exclusively in the hands of spinally injured people (Oliver and Hasler 1987).

It was not, however, as Stephen Bradshaw explains, a political organisation in the way that UPIAS and LNDP were. People were included on the basis of a common impairment, and if there was a principle on which it was based, it was that of self-help:

> It was for everybody who was spinal-cord injured. It didn't matter what your political persuasion, colour or anything else was; if you were spinal-cord injured you had certain group interests to protect in terms of the knowledge you'd gained in the spinal units, and we could all help each other and make things better for the next generation of spinal-cord injured people.

Because SIA encouraged everyone with a spinal injury to join, a wide variety of viewpoints was reflected within the organisation. This meant that it did not have a radical cutting edge, as Stephen explains:

> I obviously am concerned that SIA should be on the right side politically and be in the forefront of change, but I cannot ever see SIA being the militant front or whatever. If we took a referendum on almost any issue you like to name and if there was a radical element to it, or as soon as it began to get radical, members simply would not have voted for it.

Later, after the substantive emergence of the BCODP and the radicalisation of disability politics, single-impairment, self-help groups such as Muscle Power have taken on the 'radical element' whose absence in SIA was lamented by Stephen Bradshaw.

LOCAL STRUGGLES FOR INDEPENDENT LIVING

People were beginning to organise locally as well; mainly around local issues, anti-residential care campaigns and IL. John Evans describes the emerging situation in Hampshire:

> It was roughly about the same time as the BCODP was being formed that we had the idea of forming something like a CIL. We knew it would take time, and in a sense we still regarded Project 81 as a CIL in its infancy really. It was a scheme that was set up to enable disabled people to leave an institution and move into the community and to buy in support. It really fitted exactly the same pattern that had happened in Berkeley. Although they were university students they weren't in a residential institution like us, but they still got their act together and said 'Right, when we leave university we are going to be able to have the same support and the same assistance and we are going to be in control of that when we leave university.' It took a long time working out what we wanted to do and how we were going to do it. It took two years to get a constitution together, which was problematic, so it was all happening really at that time. I think the CIL started officially in April 1983.

In Greenwich, Rachel Hurst describes a similar process, where the focus was exclusively on local issues rather than broader ones in the emerging disability politics:

> Quite frankly half our management committee couldn't have given a damn about the politics of disability. But they did know about changing their own social climate. They did know about disabled people taking control. Our major battle in 1981 was over the setting up a residential institution in Greenwich. I was just shit scared of it. But many of our members actually wanted this 22-bedded respite-care dump they were going to spend millions on. So I'm afraid we were a little undemocratic about that. In fact we were very undemocratic about it. I think they're all very grateful about it now but at the time it wasn't easy.

Ken Davis describes the situation in Derbyshire, where the local self-organisation of disabled people probably went farther and faster than anywhere else (Davis and Mullender 1993). Residents in the local authority (LA) residential home were struggling with similar issues to those being fought in Le Court, but, on top of that, there was a local struggle over the now recognised anti-demo-cratic tendencies in DIG:

> There was the same pattern of activity there – the residents were mobilised, formed into a committee, clashed with the manage-ment committee – all the usual stuff. Then there was quite a new departure in terms of the development of the local movement – we opposed the formation of a mid-Derbyshire DIG. The local Union cell was arguing that providing people with a national disability income wasn't going to tackle the basic problem disabled people faced. But out of those public meetings to set up a mid-Derbyshire DIG there was something left behind that wouldn't go away. It was an expressed need by local disabled people for more information, because there were lots of individuals in difficulty who didn't know where to turn for solutions to their personal needs and so on. Instead of trying to carry forward the demands of the Union's political local cell, we set up an odd little organisation called DIAL [Disablement Information and Advice Line].

PROBLEMS AND CONFLICTS

It was becoming clear that some kind of co-ordinating body was going to be needed to harness all this activity, but there were a number of problems. First, there was the establishment, and the disability establishment which was meeting on a body called the Snowdon Committee. As with many similar initiatives, it had managed to obtain royal patronage through the participation of Lord Snowdon, who, despite having an interest in the lives of disabled people, knew almost nothing about the newly emerging politics of disability.

This committee had produced its own report and was despe-rately searching for a role to enable it to continue in business. Informal meetings did take place, as Patricia Rock remembers:

> Vic [Finkelstein] was speaking up and the Snowdon Committee wanted to wind down and do something else. We wanted to continue building our own organisations and we wanted to represent ourselves. Vic was very vocal at putting our views over and we were behind him. But it was said that if we continued to separate ourselves from what Lord Snowdon wanted then we wouldn't get any money. We would continue to

exist but we would really not come to anything, as we would never get any money. So we said 'Well, we'll go off on our own, we'll do our own thing and we'll represent disabled people.' We used to meet separately and we would seek money. After we had met two or three times it was clear we weren't going to get any money and they wanted us to go away. At that time there was Vic, me, Stephen Bradshaw and Alison Wertheimer from MIND.

This informal committee was a precursor of the BCODP, and already conflicts were beginning to arise. Patricia Rock describes some of these:

Vic then became the chair of this new committee which preceded the BCODP and I remember arguing, Sue [Fairclough] and I both argued, that we felt that the group was unrepresentative of women and unrepresentative of people with learning difficulties. And I remember Stephen Bradshaw speaking up and saying that he thought the main thrust of this group should be IL and housing. I really didn't feel that they were the main issues. I felt there needed to be much more political campaigning work about educating people and around actually doing a lot of direct action. That's what I wanted, and to get on the barricades. Steve and Vic were quite pally at this committee and Vic agreed that they should work on housing and IL. It's interesting that's always one of the main focuses of where the BCODP has gone, and even today, it has continued that way. Thus this agenda was set a long time ago and it's never ever really changed.

In the past, co-ordinated, collective action among disabled people had usually failed, both because the state used the tactics of 'divide and rule' and because, often, disabled people could not agree among themselves on priorities or tactics. Those attempting to organise co-ordinated activities were therefore faced with the dilemma of how much to compromise and present a united front, and how much to allow necessary and important argument full public rein. Patricia Rock was clearly not a compromiser: 'The Liberation Network was very, very strong then. They used to have enormous meetings and I refused to go to them on the grounds of the argument which said that women's politics were divisive.'

THE EMERGENCE OF THE BCODP

There are a number of different versions of how the BCODP emerged. Vic Finkelstein suggests it was a combination of the skills that had been acquired in previous years together with the theoretical base that UPIAS had established:

> I became involved with GAD when we lived there and then the Haringey one. So we were all encouraged to be active in setting up organisations. It was a tremendous learning experience. And those organisations were concerned with practical things. The idea was that the Union would be able to strengthen and help and encourage debates. So after a long period like that and some real gains both at the theory level and at the practical level, with examples like DIAL and Ken Davis's Grove Road scheme, we began to feel that we had to move on. It was in that situation that we felt that we had to get a national body together. The Union was not able to do that because it had become a focal point for developing our ideas and as a base for developing practical schemes but it wasn't going any further. We needed a national body. It was the only way to bring together existing organisations. If we had tried any other way to bring it about it would have been resisted and we already had quite a bit of experience of being resisted.

According to Maggie and Ken Davis, IYDP (International Year of Disabled People) gave impetus to the forming of a national co-ordinating body, though it was not the cause:

> In 1981 the Union members in London proposed that the only lasting contribution that the International Year might make to disabled people's lives was if we took the opportunity to try to mobilise a broader-based movement than had been possible through the Union itself. It was agreed to write a letter to all of the organisations known to us at that time inviting them to a meeting in London.

According to Vic Finkelstein, IYDP played little part in this:

> I think in 1980 we actually set up the steering group. It's quite important to say there wasn't the IYDP at that stage. The only thing that you could say about it was that we wanted it to be done by that year, but actually that thought had come before we even knew about IYDP. When we were setting up the BCODP

we made links with the existing IYDP committees because we knew they were wanting to set up a national body and retain control of it. We tried to say 'Look, you've got all these resources, why don't you put them to the BCODP.'

Some people were approached personally, as Mike Barrett recalls:

I was approached at the beginning stages by Vic as to whether we would come along to the inaugural meeting which was trying to set up the BCODP. It was to be the umbrella organisation to try and represent the collective view of disabled people in Britain on Disabled People's International [DPI].

He goes on to explain why he was interested in this new organisation:

I took along with me two of my executive members at that time because I happened to believe that it was the right way forward. I believed that we were far too fragmented. If you only look at the blind world, we have far too many blind organisations of and for in this country. When you go abroad you'll see just one, and they have achieved a lot more in certain countries than we have. They are one organisation and they get funding from the government. They may be organisations for but they still have mass memberships. Some of them could claim 60,000 or 70,000 members.

Elsa Beckett's memory is more hazy, though GEMMA became one of the founder member organisations and played a key role in the BCODP's early development:

I was doing the paper work for GEMMA, which is the disabled and able-bodied lesbian friendship network which started in 1976. I was doing all the paperwork and publicity and other bits and pieces for that – co-ordinating it all – and it was through this that I became associated with the BCODP. Sue Fairclough and I went along as representatives from GEMMA and said what we were about, and we seemed eligible to join, so we did and that's how it started.

Colin Low played little part in the emergence of the BCODP, but represented another founder member, NFB, in its early years:

I did not have a great involvement with the genesis of the

BCODP. The initiative came mainly from the recently formed UPIAS. I represented the NFB in early discussions around the constitution and for the first couple of years or so, and undertook to chair the Education Standing Committee. We agreed the objective of making the BCODP the hub of a revitalised coalition in support of integration, but I'm afraid we did not manage to take this idea very far. I think a problem for the BCODP in welding the different elements of the movement into a coherent coalition has been a lack of time on the part of the leaders of the elements of the movement which were already established to make a full input into the BCODP. This has meant that the BCODP has tended to be dominated by the interests and concerns of those less fully organised before, who took the lead in forming the BCODP, namely those with physical disabilities. I do not think that the BCODP had ever sufficiently addressed this problem, let alone successfully overcome it. Attempts have certainly been made to guarantee established organisations like those of the blind and the deaf a place at the heart of the organisation, but whether because of the calibre of the representatives sent or for whatever other reason, I do not feel these have been very successful, especially with the advent of the regional structure.

The NUD stood steadfastly aside. Paddy Ladd explains:

As to the question of how the BCODP came about, we did not wish to be involved, as we recognised some of the names of people from UPIAS in there. (Our dealing with the DA declined as we realised that the allowance they campaigned for was less and less a possibility. Our relationship with NLBD continues to be cordial to this day.)

There was more to it than personalities, however; UPIAS's uncompromising commitment to integration in all areas of life was matched by NUD's fierce determination to preserve schools for deaf people. At this point in our history, there were some compromises that could not be made. Subsequently, the BCODP has developed an inclusive education policy which is compatible with the continued existence of deaf schools.

THE INAUGURAL MEETING OF THE BCODP

People who attended this meeting have different perceptions about it. Sian Vasey 'thought that it was the most wonderful thing in the world'. Ken Davis has a similar perception:

> The meeting was held in London and the atmosphere was one of willingness to co-operate and to come together, coupled with some apprehension about the implications and the separate organisational constraints that might be around. But there was a consensus for moving forward. It was necessary to move forward and there was a major push for it, really because the requirement coming from DPI was for disabled people themselves to fill the vacuum in Britain of a national, representative organisation controlled by disabled people.

Others, like Sian, remember that discord arose over who should be sent to the First World Congress of DPI in Singapore:

> The inaugural meeting of the BCODP also selected delegates to go to Singapore and each organisation put forward a delegate. Although there was a sense of togetherness at the meeting – funnily enough – there was more of a sense of 'This really is an election', and it really was something that people were fighting their own corners for. This was healthy and people were very miffed when they didn't get selected. The LNDP, as I recall, got cross over the election procedure to go to Singapore, and it was looking as though none of their people would be going to Singapore. Then one member, I think Micheline, left the meeting and in the course of this they all said 'Oh well, we can't do anything anyway because we're not an organisation, we're just a network, so no member can represent anybody else, we are just individuals.' All this struck me as terribly interesting; all the issues of representation. I was sitting there thinking 'Oh God, this is exciting. God, this is gripping stuff.' I didn't even understand.

John Evans has a similar recollection:

> It wasn't free from having problems because I remember at one point I was wondering if that organisation would be able to be formed because at that meeting there was quite a conflict involving a number of groups who had their own interests. The LNDP all walked out at lunch time when they decided that

they didn't want anything to do with it. It wasn't a very happy start to what I thought should be the national disability organisation. There were all these fights starting off already before we were able to make a proper start. However, having said that, it's interesting now to see a lot of those people who were part of that Liberation Network who walked out that day are all very active in the movement. It's come round in a complete full circle, and they're all doing their own thing in different ways, and it's worked, but there are still those conflicts.

NOT EVERYONE AGREES

Once it was agreed that the organisation was to be formed and that it would be called the British Council of Organisations of Disabled People, there came the issue of who should be included and excluded and on what grounds. Stephen Bradshaw recalls:

I remember the first meeting. There were those people who were for and those who were against including certain groups. Some were saying 'Well you can't exclude the RADARs of this world, that's where all the power is and you can't expect to get anywhere without having a system for including them.' I remember that it was quite clear and obvious that it was only organisations of disabled people who operate on a national basis were going to have votes because they were virtually the only ones who existed at that time. There were also one or two other small local organisations and that seemed quite straight-forward that those groups should vote.

Even though Mike Barrett was supportive, he had problems with his own executive's various prejudices:

The trouble was that we got bedded down with the problems of deciding who was going to be entitled to become affiliates to the BCODP, and we got bogged down in the arguments about lesbian and gay issues among other things, and it put my two executive members off. They went back to the executive and talked about it and the executive just threw it out. I kept on ever since then to make them become affiliates and finally I won the day. I made them realise that this was an organisation which we should join.

According to Stephen Bradshaw, from the outset the BCODP was going to be an organisation which stuck to its principles, even if this may have demonstrated, as he claims, a certain naivety:

> We were politically very naive in terms of how we were getting ahead, but of course when you've got lots of people who haven't had a decent education, haven't experienced the organisational context or had the ability to attract money, what do you cling to other than your principles? So it was very understandable that we were relatively naive in the way we operated, because the principles were the most important thing that you could have.

While this was frustrating at times, he relates how the pragmatic approach won out concerning the issue of whether to apply for charitable status or not:

> In terms of the organisation trying to be extremely highly principled and idealistic, we spent an immense amount of time arguing about whether it should be a charity or not. Eventually a pragmatic approach was adopted which said 'OK, we know where we're going, we know we're compromising, but the compromise has to be that we become a charity because if we don't, we're not going to get anywhere in terms of being able to influence or change things within the foreseeable future, because we're not going to get any money or support without this little tag called charity.'

Despite pragmatism triumphing over principle in this particular case, recognition and resources were still slow in arriving, as Elsa Beckett recounts:

> At first we didn't seem to get any recognition. I can remember writing more or less begging letters to try and get some start-up money from organisations like Tate and Lyle and Barclays Bank. We used to get a hundred pounds here and a hundred there, and this was just to cover our start-up expenses. It really was a struggle. Well even now we're not getting the money that the group needs. It's because of the entrenched, established groups. That's where the difficulty in being recognised lies. People keep saying 'You've got RADAR, you've got this, you've got that, what do you need the BCODP for?'. I don't know if it's just the British atmosphere around disability and it's the way

we present ourselves, perhaps. It seems to me that in the States they're louder in some ways than we are.

Pragmatism and political compromises were something that the BCODP continued to struggle with as the campaign for civil rights gained momentum in the UK.

CONCLUSIONS: IS THE BCODP THE EMERGING DISABILITY MOVEMENT?

Having described the way in which the BCODP emerged, the final issues we need to consider in this chapter are twofold: does the BCODP constitute the disability movement itself, and does its arrival signify that the emerging movement amongst disabled people has finally emerged?

Judy Hunt, in thinking about the first of these issues, comes to a similar conclusion to ours:

> Looking at the BCODP as the major focus, I certainly feel that it's been the point at which the movement became very visible and took on board the social interpretation of disability, but it was also the outcome of what had gone before. In a sense it was the build-up that began to take place in the 1970s and in the 1960s that was crucial.

We agree; we do not suggest that the disability movement and the BCODP are the same thing. Rather, the BCODP became the formal organisational focus for a range of issues including critiques of state-based and voluntary-sector-based welfare, struggles for IL, campaigns against discrimination in all its forms, self-help, and challenges to the negative imagery and stereotypes with which disabled people constantly have to live.

In respect of the second of these issues, observers of social movements suggest that the transition from emerging to emergent movement is signified when the movement becomes larger, less spontaneous, better organised, and led by formal structures rather than ad hoc committees and informal groups. In these terms and at this point in its history, the BCODP has some way to go before we can suggest that its establishment signifies that the emerging movement has emerged. This is the issue that we will describe and discuss in more detail in the next chapter.

Chapter 5

Organising disabled people

Without democracy, there can be no politics, and without a genuine and inclusive politics, the claims of the disempowered will not be heard.

(Friedman 1992: 135)

INTRODUCTION

In this chapter the emergence of the BCODP will be described and many of the initial difficulties it encountered in its struggles to survive in the 1980s will be discussed. Its links with DPI, which emerged at the same time, will be considered as will the mushrooming of local organisations of disabled people. All this will be located in the context of attempts by the disability establishment to undermine this emergent organisation. The significance of its survival will also be discussed.

THE ARRIVAL OF THE BCODP

The emergence of the BCODP as a democratic, accountable and representative organisation with a broad approach to disability was bound to have an impact on campaigning organisations such as NLBD. Mike Barrett, for example, recognises the limitation of his organisation's approach as a single-issue, single-impairment grouping:

> In the early days we were lobbying for better employment opportunity, sheltered workshops being the foremost goal. Our rules have always said that we wanted to see equality in all areas of work and our object was to see opportunities in all fields including the professional ones. But our main thrust

came from the workshops. We also fought hard for benefits and all those sorts of issues.

However, he also points out that the historical roots of direct action and political protest can be located in the development of his own organisation:

We carried out a march of blind people from Wales and the north, north west and coming up from the south west, and we all congregated in Trafalgar Square in 1920. That was the push that got the final piece of legislation on the statute book. We used a motto then – 'Rights not charity'. You can see it in the photographs that we've got, they show the fact that we were using these slogans way back in those years gone by.

The BCODP's emergence was also bound to have an effect on the existing disability establishment organisations, which, up to now, had enjoyed a cosy relationship with the government and state. Phillip Mason draws a sharp contrast between the existing, traditional, rich and non-accountable organisations and the newly emerging ones which were struggling to survive financially. Two contrasting meetings were the basis for a comparison:

I had been to a meeting at the Cheshire Foundation. It was full of these noble do-gooders; men, mainly elderly and mainly military, air force or navy – the sherry was flowing, the room was full of smoke and they just stood around. It was just totally repulsive. The affluence that was exhibited was really, really disgusting. The BCODP meeting was so different. It was poverty, real poverty. It was a grotty, dark hall as I remember it. When you just think of disabled people and how they used to meet. It's a disgrace really.

In the previous chapter we mentioned the Snowdon Committee. It was very concerned at the existence of the BCODP. Vic Finkelstein recalls:

We had some telephone calls and I think Stephen [Bradshaw] must have spoken to him [Lord Snowdon] on the phone. He was just hysterical. We were trying to calm him down, saying 'We're not opposed to what you're doing, we just want disabled people to control it, that's all.' But they were just adamant. Again, for me it was a surprise, because I really couldn't understand why there was this violent opposition to disabled people controlling their own affairs. And I thinks it's been consistent ever since.

And, as a South African, he professes to be perplexed at the opposition that the BCODP engendered:

It's English culture, I suppose. I don't quite understand what it's all about. It didn't bother me particularly at the time. It was just like earlier on, when someone like Peter Townsend didn't come out in full support of the Union. If he'd been more foresightful he should have supported us. They [DA] really should have supported us. We had a lot to bring – if they'd thrown in their lot with us it would have been a different situation altogether. We really made a lot of effort to talk to other key people like Selwyn Goldsmith, Bert Massey and the transport people [the Joint Committee on Mobility].

THE INFLUENCE OF DPI

The DPI emerged in the same year as the BCODP, out of the anger of 200 disabled delegates at a two-and-a-half-thousand strong Rehabilitation International [RI] conference in Winnipeg. Disabled delegates were outraged at the decision *not* to ensure disabled people's representation on the IYDP organising committee. In protest they walked out, and the now Director of DPI, Henry Enns, addressed the boycott of disabled people, who came from over thirty countries, saying: 'Do I hear you want to form your own international organisation of disabled people?'.

There was a resounding 'Yes!' to this question, without a single dissension. He then called upon delegates to go back to their respective countries and start a national assembly of disabled people that could feed into an international body.

It is not easy to assess the influence of DPI on the emergence of the BCODP. Certainly some of the key participants were aware of its existence; Mike Barrett, for example:

I knew and was aware of DPI before the BCODP and I knew that DPI had started because of the battle within Rehabilitation International. Disabled people were saying that it was very much being run by the able-bodied and they wanted to really do something about it. They decided that they wanted to start up an organisation which would be for disabled people which could rival Rehabilitation International.

Stephen Bradshaw describes how a visit to the United States at that time opened his eyes to the conflict in Rehabilitation International and the emergence of DPI:

> Going back to the beginnings of the BCODP, at that time I was going on a trip to the States which was quite an eye-opener for me, because that's when I actually found out about DPI; how that year at the Rehabilitation International Conference in Winnipeg all these disabled people got together and lobbied. I thought, 'God, you know this is quite something.' Before I went to the States I'd been in touch with Vic Finkelstein, and he said 'When you're in the States go and meet Ed Roberts.' He gave me a few other people to go and visit as well. So when I was out there, obviously as well as researching, I was finding out about DPI and the planning of the First World Congress in Singapore. And, of course, we never had anything that could fit into it. We never had a British organisation that could fit, so it was quite a concern. Behind the scenes there was a lot of thinking being done, and the Union especially were quite active, but I remember Ed Roberts said 'You've got to go back and something's got to happen in England. You've really got to get your organisation together to become part of this.' And when I came back the speed of change and the speed of organisation were incredible. Within a few weeks of coming back there was the initial meeting that happened in Kilburn, in that old beaten-up school, with all the organisations the Union had called together. All in all there were about twelve or thirteen organisations that came together to set up the BCODP.

In fact it was seven organisations that formed the steering group which constituted the BCODP. Only national organisations could join at the outset. Membership was extended to local organisations, including Derbyshire Centre for Integrated Living (DCIL) and GAD, nine months later in 1982.

However, Vic Finkelstein is adamant that DPI merely helped and gave legitimacy to something which would have happened anyway:

> I think we would have got it anyway. Indeed there was some debate about whether we actually should join DPI or whether

we should concentrate on building our own national organisation. My argument was that we should not have a narrow view;
that maintaining links with DPI would broaden our view, give
us some experience of other contexts and the DPI could support
us. And our involvement then could feed into them. In absolute
terms I don't think that it made much difference. Later on
towards the end of the time when I was Chair, when people like
Henry Enns started visiting Britain, then I think people started
becoming more interested. At the beginning, the BCODP was
held together by myself, Dick Leaman, Francine White and Elsa
Beckett, and various others such as Peter Large and Colin Low
participated then. As long as we held the organisations in the
BCODP, we would have carried on. My view at the time was
'The longer we can hold this together the longer it is likely to
survive.' So I would see the DPI connection as just strengthening, reinforcing, but not a crucial factor.

But, according to Vic Finkelstein, the existence of DPI was very
helpful in establishing the credibility of the BCODP. Without it,
what group could have represented disabled people from Britain
at the First World Congress of DPI?

But where DPI helped us in the BCODP, in my view, was in the
arguments as to why disabled people needed to control their
own affairs in a co-ordinated way in Britain. When we
presented those arguments to Snowdon or any of the other
people we would say, 'Look, they're doing it all around the
world', and in that respect it was a help. It was very important.

He goes on to make the point that the existence of DPI not only
gave credibility to what was happening in Britain, but that
participation in international developments was very empowering for those who were involved, particularly for himself, Stephen
Bradshaw and Francine White, who attended the First World
Congress on behalf of the BCODP: 'Because Stephen, Francine and
I participated in debates, it meant that when we came back and
when I talked to people – and I'm sure Stephen and Francine
talked to people too – you just felt that much more confident.'

The British contingent worked hard and made a significant
impact at the Congress.itself. Stephen Bradshaw describes his
experience:

Of course, we arrived at Singapore and found that we were

probably the only country that had done things correctly, but it was the First World Congress. It was very significant because it got us to act quicker, we had to resolve things and so that got us moving and got us more on the map than a lot of people believed possible.

Coming back after the exhilaration of Singapore only served to reinforce the realisation of just how much needed to be done at home:

After that it was really this awful hard slog. Meeting after meeting with not that much being achieved. We were really struggling to keep going, to get more people, to try and work out a system that would actually enable us to reach out to more and more disabled people.

However, the Second World Congress came round four years later with the BCODP not only still in existence but able to send a bigger contingent this time:

The Second World Congress was something to be working for and lots more people went out that time rather than the three that went out to Singapore. So a lot more people became aware of the international issues and the significance of DPI. It was again tremendously empowering and strengthening when you get international groups of disabled people together as in Singapore and the Bahamas. Those who were lucky enough to go did feel a sense of power, and one saw that in the Bahamas and one saw it again in Vancouver [at the Third World Congress]. I think Vancouver will be another milestone in the BCODP because, again, that many more people have been exposed to the power of disabled people internationally, and now we've got representative status at the UN, we're actually doing things.

THE IDEA OF AN ORGANISATION OF OUR OWN

In the early years, it was the idea that was the glue that held the organisation together; it certainly was not a solid financial base or its achievements in terms of material gains for disabled people. Micheline Mason captures this perfectly:

The idea of the BCODP is more important to me than the real

thing. I have pondered long on why this should be. One reason is that you cannot join the BCODP unless you happen to have access to a self-governed organisation, and not all of these organisations are exactly exciting to belong to, so lots of unorganised disabled people are still without a 'democratic' means of representation. Until very recently I was in this position myself.

It was important for the BCODP's democratic, representative strength to confine the membership to organisations of disabled people. The policy encouraged disabled individuals to join forces and establish groups where their power would increase. It also stimulated the takeover by disabled people of their local organisations for disabled people that were traditionally run by able-bodied philanthropists. Fourteen years later, with a membership of over 110 separate organisations, the BCODP has felt confident enough to open up membership to individuals.

Also, in its early years, its frailty was, ironically, a major strength – to cough too loud might have destroyed the whole organisation. Phillip Mason draws an apposite analogy:

> It was very frail. At the inaugural meeting, Vic Finkelstein was there and Vic's voice is a very frail voice. So there was a sense that – this is a very frail, very fragile, precious thing. But there was also a mystery about it, you know. What is it? I didn't have a clear understanding.

We did have some understanding, however, of what we were doing and not doing; according to Phillip Mason:

> We knew what it was not about. We knew that it wasn't about do-gooders deciding what 1981 was about. To some extent that was a politicising influence, although we didn't see it in that sense. In Hampshire we already had a strong sense about 1981; that it should be something for disabled people and that whatever happened should be driven by disabled people.

The idea, once given life, was not going to be allowed to die, as Elsa Beckett reminds us:

> The determination of everybody there to keep going no matter what the struggle, even if we didn't get any funding, we would have kept going as a pressure group if nothing else. People did seem so determined. I didn't get the impression that anybody

was contemplating saying 'Oh dear, if we don't get any money we'll fold up.' I never got that impression.

The simple idea of disabled people controlling their own lives, emerging from the earlier intellectual work of UPIAS and others, has, suggests Rachel Hurst, brought incalculable benefits which last even to today:

> I think the debt we owe the thinkers from the 1970s is incalculable, and when I look at the BCODP in relation to other movements throughout the world, we are far and away, without any question of a shadow of a doubt, the most articulate around disability. It was so clear in Vancouver, quite invigorating actually. We may have not got very far as a movement with money and all the rest of it but, by God, we know what we're at. We actually really do clearly understand the definition of disability.

A PLATFORM FOR CHANGE

If all that had happened was that we had succeeded in keeping an idea alive, there would not be much to feel pleased about. As Karl Marx remarked: 'Philosophers have interpreted the world, the real point is to change it.' So how responsible has the BCODP been in changing the disability status quo? Maggie and Ken Davis list some real changes that have emerged directly from the BCODP. The first was to demedicalise the draft constitution of DPI, which had originally been based on the World Health Organisation classification (Wood 1980):

> The major thing to establish was a proper focus based on the social approach to disability. That first struggle came from the BCODP and was taken into DPI. A lot of pressure was put on the DPI delegates to push forward the draft constitution of DPI in its original form, which had a medical model definition in its preamble. It was something which our people worked ever so hard to correct and did in fact bring about, which was a major success. The very first major success for the British movement; we won the battle of ideas which lay at the heart of the movement itself.

In addition, they suggest that the very existence of the BCODP has changed the political and disability establishments irrevocably:

The existence of a focal point for the movement itself meant that for the very first time in Britain, disabled people themselves had come together in a collective sense at the heart of disability politics in Britain. They had mounted a clear challenge to everything that had gone before. The social approach to disability was, in itself, a political challenge not just to society to change but to all of the controllers of disability policy. Giving notice to them that from that moment on they were under pressure for change and that their legitimacy was under challenge. How can anybody measure the success of that kind of development?

That is not to say that these two establishments did not attempt to fight back. By 1985, when the BCODP had firmly established itself on the scene, there was a proposal to establish a national disability council which had some fairly strong support. The BCODP was adamantly against it, building on the lessons from UPIAS that sticking to principles was crucial rather than opportunistically seizing on any chance that materialised. In addition, as Rachel Hurst recalls, DPI connection was also significant:

It was in 1985 that there was the big difficult problem around Lord Henderson's national council. It was a major battle, but because we were a part of DPI, we were able to resist. I think our connection with DPI was absolutely crucial. It gave us credibility. As I think it did for many organisations throughout the world.

The BCODP quickly adopted the social model as the basis for organising its own activities, which gave it credibility among other disability organisations and assisted in their development. Sian Vasey suggests that this was important, as was the chance for disabled people to meet together:

So it was the social model around which we organised. More recently we've organised National Disability Arts Forum along the same model. I see the BCODP's success, in a way, just in its being. I know this is a bizarre thing to say, but the fact that it facilitates an annual gathering of disabled people is not something one should just minimise. I don't think you can say that there haven't been any successes until ADL comes about, and in some way it is transparently clear that it is the BCODP that is responsible for ADL. I think it's going to be a problem when

ADL does come about because everybody's going to claim it for themselves.

Ann MacFarlane agrees with the latter point and suggests that the BCODP has played a role in building a collective identity amongst disabled people:

Well I do see the BCODP as the focus and I think the BCODP's good points are that it's certainly got the debate going where there was no debate before. It's brought many disabled people together and given them a sense of identity and a sense of belonging, however tenuous that is. And I think it's begun to do some really good work. In the last two or three years we've seen a real shift and there's been some really good pieces of work, like the ADL campaign and the Colin Barnes book [Barnes 1991].

ORGANISING THE GRASSROOTS

Probably the most exciting development in disabled people's self-organisation in recent years has been the growth of local, democratic organisations of disabled people. Again, according to Patricia Rock, the BCODP must take a great deal of credit for this:

I think the BCODP is coming into its own time, it's also done very, very good groundwork. It's a representative body. I'm now a representative and I wouldn't have been if I didn't think the BCODP was a representative organisation. I actually think it's taken its grass roots seriously.

Maggie and Ken Davis suggest that the existence of the BCODP gives credibility to local groups wishing to self-organise democratically in exactly the same way as DPI gave credibility to the BCODP at the national level:

Another major success is the immeasurable penetration into the movement of local organisations of disabled people and the fact that they are now able to claim that they are not isolated any more; that they are part of a national expression of disabled people's will; that they aren't a local group of unrepresentative individuals crying in the wind. And again, who can measure the depth of that success?

Micheline Mason adds another dimension to this:

The BCODP also acts as an incentive to local groups of disabled people to become self-governing. As most of us are still desperately needing to 'belong' to something, the idea of being excluded from our own 'umbrella' is too much to bear, and so we will do what it takes to qualify for membership. This is not a bad thing at this point in time.

And its existence, according to Millie Hill, also got the attention of local politicians, policy makers and service providers:

It's made a hell of a lot of difference, because the profile of disabled people and disability issues has gone way up the agenda in Hammersmith and Fulham in terms of services that have been provided, and in terms of meetings with councillors to raise their awareness. Whereas when the Hammersmith and Fulham Association was being run by non-disabled people, disability was way down at the bottom of the agenda, and there's nothing like actually being confronted by a group of angry disabled people. The impact is different than if it was a non-disabled person coming along to say 'This is what you should be doing for disabled people.' When it's actually disabled people speaking for themselves, it makes a difference.

By now the relationship between the national and the local has become a symbiotic one. Rachel Hurst puts it this way:

The turning point for the survival was the growth of the small local organisations and the fact that the membership shot up every year, almost doubling itself; certainly every two years it doubled itself. These organisations really did have some political knowledge.

Finally, Patricia Rock suggests that the existence of such an extensive network of local organisations will keep the organisation safe, as its leaders get their hands dirty at the national political level:

Without parliamentary impetus, without trying to get recognition at that level, then the BCODP won't survive. It won't survive to get its policy and practices implemented. It won't survive in terms of getting enough funding to support the number of organisations that are now beginning to join. I think that we are now in a position where we can compete on a national level because there's a very good internal structure of regionalisation. The BCODP is really getting its house in order.

ONGOING DIFFICULTIES

Two of the major problems that have been around since the inception of the BCODP have been its chronic lack of resources and the antipathy, not to say downright opposition, that its very presence has engendered amongst the disability establishment; that is, the traditional organisations for disabled people. Ann MacFarlane puts it thus:

> There is a certain frustration in the fact that because the BCODP has been so poorly resourced, woefully, inadequately resourced, just like any movement or any organisation, people start to get frustrated. There's unrest and you start to see other groups getting frustrated and thinking 'I'll go off and do my own thing.' That has a bit of a concern for me because, at almost the same time, traditional charities have done their best to weaken us, to weaken the BCODP.

While some of this antipathy may have been resolved in recent co-operation over civil rights legislation (Oliver and Barnes 1995), the fact remains that the BCODP and the disability establishment are in direct competition for financial support. In terms of government Section 64 funding,[1] for example, the BCODP's main competitor, RADAR, receives eight times more.

Jenny Morris reflects on these issues in terms of trying to organise a conference involving both sets of competing interests:

> That was my first contact with the BCODP and I must say that the process of organising the conference was dire. And the BCODP was partly responsible for making it dire. The Prince of Wales Advisory Group was much more responsible. They behaved just appallingly, but actually the main reason they behaved appallingly was that they were petrified of the BCODP. The Director of the Group just got cold feet about being associated with this radical organisation, and in the end they pulled their name off the conference and just said that it was a Living Options project.

She goes on to relate this to the disparities in the finances of both groups:

The BCODP has great difficulties because it is essentially competing with very wealthy organisations, and it's very easy for the BCODP to appear to be inadequate and inefficient in comparison with those organisations. And unfortunately that is how it appears a lot of the time.

And she relates this back to the idea of the BCODP being very important, even if the reality is less than perfect:

When you send off money and you don't get anything in return, it feels like a void. That's what the BCODP feels like a lot of the time to me. It feels like a void. I'm very glad it's there but, as I said, my contact with it over the conference was very, very difficult and it just drove me up the wall as an organisation.

Phillip Mason suggests two further difficulties. First, there is the issue of how much the BCODP has been able to set its own agenda, and second, that of how much it has been forced to respond to agendas set by others:

The BCODP hasn't been able to set its own agenda and work to it. To some extent it's had to respond; it's had to be reactive rather than proactive simply because that's how disabled people have been treated in the last ten years. We've been pulled and pushed around all over the place. And you tend to have to run to the tune of the paymaster or mistress. That's the sad thing and therefore it can't pretend to have been all the things that it would have liked to have been.

While there may be some truth in this, we suggested earlier that one of the strengths of the BCODP, having learned lessons from UPIAS, was that it did stick to its principles; often to the point where outsiders criticised it for being too negative and refusing to involve itself in current issues and concerns.

A second question Phillip Mason raises is how well the BCODP has been able to communicate its ideas to all disabled people:

Perhaps if the BCODP has failed it is perhaps because it hasn't necessarily got its message across to ordinary disabled people. It talks about anti-discrimination legislation when many disabled people really don't know what it means. There is a danger that politicised people within the BCODP, including myself, aren't speaking a language that's understandable by ordinary disabled people. And, in fact, people might feel antagonistic towards what we're saying. When the BCODP started there was a lot of bad feeling amongst disabled people. When somebody stood up the front and said 'I'm proud to be disabled', lots of people in the room didn't understand, didn't feel it. But then that's a growth process.

Again, not everyone would agree with that. Patricia Rock suggests that one of the BCODP's major strengths is its non-elitism:

I think one of its most recent successes is to take a non-elitist approach. At the Personal Assistance Users conference I was very impressed by some of the people coming. One of the chaps in my workshop was leaving an institution the following week and he'd been in an institution for thirty years. I think that if you can get sort of people like that to come along, people who have never spoken up, who are the mainstream of disabled people, then the organisation must be actually having an impact at quite a deep grassroots level.

And Millie Hill explains how, in contrast to some disability organisations in Canada, the BCODP has managed to maintain an interest in issues relevant to the lives of disabled individuals:

Although I was involved with disability organisations in Canada, issues around things like personal assistance I didn't know anything about until I came to Britain. There were things that weren't talked about even within disability circles in Canada, at least not the ones that I was involved with. For example, the right of disabled people to take control of their lives, that came to me about three or four years ago.

Nasa Begum is worried that the movement is more concerned about formal, organised meetings than providing personal support to, and education for, each other:

We are still very much a meetings culture. I don't know, maybe it's something about the special schools system or whatever. Disabled people don't seem to get together as much socially to develop support systems with each other. There's very little discussion, so unless you have already sussed it out or can understand all the books, there's very little to actually give you access to learning about some of the issues.

She goes on to suggest that part of the reason for this is the kind of education that is provided for disabled people:

> A lot of disabled people learn stuff as a student. You come across feminism or the class does some of the race stuff. You get a bit of the black civil rights stuff as a student and become more political. But there's nothing in terms of disability. So there's no conversations, no discussion about what's happening, what's going on with disabled people. I just find that there is a real need for some of that to actually give people access.

Rachel Hurst suggests that meetings themselves have often been a problem:

> One of our problems that we've had, and are still having, was that Council was reinventing or changing agreed decisions at nearly every council meeting. This was because there were new people coming along and each time you had to start from scratch. It may not be so bad with regionalisation. It wasn't so bad in the early stages because there were a hard core of people who kept at it month after month.

Because of the flexibility and fluidity of evolving organisational structures in emerging social movements and the constant influx of new people, it is not unusual for such happenings to occur.

THE INDIVIDUAL AND THE COLLECTIVE

An issue which confronts all organisations as they evolve, not just new social movements, is that of the relationship between the individual and the collective. Jenny Morris warns:

> I think you have to be careful. I am only an individual. I only speak as an individual. I've got no desire to be a representative of an organisation. As an individual I have as much right as anybody else to contribute to the debate. I'm not claiming to represent people, all I'm doing is representing my own opinion.

Sian Vasey, on the other hand, points out that the BCODP is, after all, an organisation:

> The disability movement is something more than the sum of its membership. It's an organisation and although organisations

have members, they also have structures. In involving disabled people, I don't see how else it can formally be done.

This further raises the question of whom the BCODP represents at both the individual and collective level. Phillip Mason ponders his own involvement: 'I remember thinking "What's a nice little middle-class boy like me doing here?".' And Mike Barrett voices an often-heard criticism: 'The image that the BCODP has got with many disability groups is it's the wheelchair brigade.' Rachel Hurst takes this point further and reflects on the issues it raises for the movement in general:

> One of the things we have to look at and be confident about is the reality of why most leaders in the disability movement are wheelchair users. It is very important that the movement has representation from every one of the major impairments. But we as a movement, and this is not just the BCODP, it's DPI as well, have to acknowledge it.

Clearly, following the social model, the disabling barriers to political participation are less severe for wheelchair users than for people with other impairments. It is no small challenge to the movement to attempt to ensure that these barriers are eradicated so that no impairment groups are disadvantaged.

Mike Barrett emphasises the need for understanding amongst all disabled people about the nature of different impairments:

> Let me put it this way. I personally think that the BCODP is a necessity, but I still think it has a lot of things it's got to do. It's got to help every one of us to understand each other's impairments and be able to understand those properly so we can put them in their right context. For each impairment is unique to its own group of people. There are many people who will say that the blind person is not disabled. I've had that said to me by a number of forthright wheelchair users.

The growth of the BCODP also led to questions of democratic accountability and issues about who is entitled to speak for whom. Again, Mike Barrett explains:

> A problem with the BCODP was that, in its early years, before it had a full-time director and before it had its funding and it was feeling its way, it started to make statements in the press which caused aggravation because no one had been consulted about

what sort of statement, or what sort of response we were going to give to certain things that were happening.

And it should be remembered that not all groups would see the BCODP as being central to their struggles, as representatives of People First made clear when we met them: 'I don't know. I don't think they've ever heard of the BCODP.' People First joined the BCODP in 1994. Both organisations are going through a tremendous learning curve, and tensions, due to prejudices and historical oppression, still run high. As Simone Aspis candidly writes:

> People with learning difficulties face discrimination in the disability movement. People without learning difficulties use the medical model when dealing with us. We are always asked to talk about advocacy and our impairments as though our barriers aren't disabling in the same way as disabled people without learning difficulties. We want concentration on our access needs in the mainstream disability movement.

Simone thinks the lack of true collaboration between people with and without learning difficulties stems from a fear in the latter of being labelled 'stupid, thick, mental and mad' by the non-disabled public. Therefore if people with and without learning difficulties were seen together, the stereotype of disabled people as incapable would be enhanced. Simone suggests that equality within the disability movement will only truly be achieved when people with learning difficulties are given positions of power and influence within the movement: 'We look forward to the day when a person with learning difficulties will be elected to represent all disabled people's interests, like chair or spokesperson.'

Here Simone raises an important issue around representation and the legitimacy of various spokespeople – in other words, whom should the BCODP speak for? Vic Finkelstein is forthright about this:

> We shouldn't deny that it is a minority of disabled people who belong to the BCODP. If you say there are 7 million disabled people in Britain, obviously only a tiny minority are politically active in disability movement. We shouldn't deny that. The BCODP reflects a tiny minority, but the Thatcher government was elected on a minority of the electorate.

Colin Low responds differently to the same issue:

I'm not sure how far it can truly be said that the BCODP is representative of the mass of disabled people. The emphasis on the social origins of disability to the exclusion of individual aspects and an interactive approach, the emphasis on rights rather than services, and the rhetorical style have not been sufficiently talked through, and would probably fail to carry large sections of the disabled population. The building of a broadly based and democratic mass movement is a constant prey to frustration and distracting compromise, and requires the tolerance and accommodation of many divergent points of view. I'm not sure how far the BCODP has had the patience for this.

Richard Wood is adamant that the key factor that separates the BCODP from other disability organisations is that it was built by disabled people, it exists because of disabled people, and if we withdrew support from it, it would cease to exist:

It's unquestionably true that it's what we've created. That's the unique thing about it. Nobody has elevated the BCODP to this position of – in the same way as, say, DIAL UK has elevated itself into a position of first creating the organisation and then saying it's the national one. The BCODP has not self-elevated itself. It is where it is because disabled people ask it to be there. If disabled people didn't want it to be there they could dismantle it again.

One could ask how many other disability organisations are in the same position, or indeed how many already exist which have little or no support from disabled people at all.

DOES THE BCODP REPRESENT EVERYONE?

The issue of representation leads on to the crucial issue of whether the BCODP is the disability movement or whether it is part of something broader. Micheline Mason suggests:

For me, the BCODP is only part of the disability movement, albeit a vital part. The most important thing about its existence is the statement it makes about our right to self-representation. It is also a huge contradiction to our isolation and individual-ism. The development of the disability arts movement is contributing greatly to the reclaiming of our self-esteem and pride as disabled people, and, as a parent of a disabled child, I am excited at the realisation that she is growing up with the positive 'role models' we all needed and none of us had, and a culture of her own. This is a new world we are building.

And she goes on to explain why she believes the movement is, and must remain, broader than a single organisation:

The reason is my fear of not being allowed to think new thoughts. I have never been attracted to organisations which demand loyalty to a 'party' line without the recognition that 'truth' is evolving – being discovered all the time. Very few associations of people have managed to be both committed to a common philosophy or programme, and at the same time encourage and support individual development or creativity. The disability movement has not found a way yet, particularly to be welcoming to internal debate. Perhaps our unity still feels too new and fragile to too many people to take such risks. Small, local debating groups may be an answer.

AN ALTERNATIVE APPROACH

Not everyone would agree that the attempt to create and build our own organisations has necessarily been the right or most effective way to proceed. Colin Low has taken issue with this position from our first contact with him:

Your paper speaks of the new movement being built in the teeth of opposition from the traditional voluntary organisations. This would have been true of the blind world until the mid-1970s. However, as a result of the strategy of infiltrating and taking over the organisations for the blind, particularly the RNIB, adopted by the organisations of blind people from the early 1970s, this has not been the case in the blind world for the last fifteen years, and the RNIB has supported the growth of blind organisations and the policies/campaigning objectives they have favoured.

He goes on to argue the case for creating broad alliances between representative and non-representative organisations:

The organisations of blind people have accepted that power, resources and expertise resided in the traditional voluntary organisations. They recognised that this was not something which was going to be turned round overnight and that it was necessary to work with this situation and direct it to their own ends. This has inclined them towards a more coalition style of politics which recognised that disabled people needed allies, and that it was necessary for them to work with able-bodied people and with existing institutions if they were to get anywhere. The BCODP has adopted a more straightforwardly oppositional stance which, I would argue, has not only secured fewer gains, but has also meant that the disability movement has been divided in its approach.

A POLITICS OF WHAT?

There is a final issue that needs to be considered: the role of the disability movement (and indeed the disability establishment) in wider aspects of British politics. Britain is what might be called a representative democracy, in which a variety of groups, interests and parties is accorded legitimacy to speak on behalf of whole constituencies or groups of interest. But representation in representative democracy is always considerably less than perfect, as Vic Finkelstein points out:

> My position was that in a representative democracy where people organise and present their views, you take those views to represent the group they say they're representing until other organisations emerge to challenge them. That's what democracy is about. Inasmuch as there is no other reflection of their views, these are the views. The fact that it's a minority membership is true, but the question then is 'Who speaks for the majority?'. I once gave a talk to a medical disability group and they raised this issue. They said, 'These views you're putting forward are interesting, but they only represent a minority of disabled people. So I said, 'Who represents the majority? You?'. Of course, they just became embarrassed, because if it isn't us it's them, the doctors.

Or, one might add, the disability establishment.

Stephen Bradshaw makes the argument that the politics of disability is about human rights and therefore transcends narrow partisan arguments about the left and right:

Whether we're using left-wing analysis or Marxist analysis or whatever analysis it is, it doesn't matter. The thing is that we're getting together, and whatever structures we use to help us change things, the principal thing is that we're getting together and that's the core of what we're doing. We're getting together not to air our political views or try and make the world this or that in terms of left- or right-wing politics. We're there to make it different in terms of the politics of disability, which is about the rights of individuals; it is about us having the ability to control our own lives. We can do that in a right-wing society, we can do that in a left-wing society. So I'd still say the BCODP is too much still giving the impression of being left-wing. Not consciously but I think unconsciously. Because of the historical past, it does need to concentrate on the human rights issues – whether it's left-wing rights or right-wing rights doesn't matter.

Rachel Hurst suggests that at the local level, organisations of disabled people have to work with the political parties in power and other power structures as well:

It was also a very pragmatic issue. It was quite clear also that it was the local organisations, like Derbyshire, like Greenwich, that were providing the major backbone of people with the experience of working with politicians and others in power.

THE BCODP BY THE END OF THE DECADE

So far in this chapter we have attempted to look at the emergence of the BCODP and some of the key issues that confronted it in the first ten years. In reflecting on where the BCODP has come from, John Evans makes a number of very important points. First, he suggests that the BCODP provided a network and organisational structure to enable disabled people to become a political force:

I think is important, when you set up an organisation like the BCODP, that it provides a networking system that can put organisations of disabled people doing similar things in touch with each other, and as a means of communication, as a means of working, politicising ourselves. Even when it comes to organising demonstrations, organising lobbies, organising some sort of political activity, we have got the structure, the focus – by having that network all organised under the umbrella of the BCODP.

In addition, as well as for the other reasons we have already discussed, he suggests that the individual participants were the key to the slow start in building the organisation:

It took a long time getting that organisational structure together, but one of the reasons for that is most of the key activists involved in setting up were all very busy themselves. They were, and are, the main resources and their time was limited, and so I think that's why things only started moving properly in the mid-1980s.

Finally, he concludes that by the end of the 1980s the BCODP had emerged as the legitimate voice of disabled people:

The BCODP is the organisation, it is the voice. It was set up to be the voice of disabled people in this country, and because of its democratic development, its democratic structure, it has been able to become that.

As well as the BCODP being the voice of disabled people, Phillip Mason argues that it has raised the profile of disabled people and disability issues considerably:

Well it's raised the profile of disabled people in society. There is no doubt about that at all. Absolutely no doubt at all. It grew because it had a basic, fundamental truth, which was that disabled people must speak and act for themselves. It kept on saying that, and gradually disabled people identified with the value and the truth of it, and it's grown in strength because of that. It's raised the profile of disabled people in society. It's also given disabled people confidence. Disabled people in the community have come into their own at the end of the 1980s because the critical mass was able to coalesce round the BCODP.

According to Rachel Hurst, the BCODP has raised this profile internationally as well:

It provided a focus for the growth of organisations and because of it, its links with DPI and the work that it did internationally and the profile that it then gave us at an international level were very important.

Elsa Beckett, on the other hand, provides a different response: 'The BCODP doesn't come into my consciousness terribly other than as a good thing to say, to be brutally frank.'

CONCLUSIONS

There is no doubt that the BCODP has now taken on many of the characteristics that make emerging social movements emergent. By the end of the 1980s, it was much larger, had a formal structure, and had links both down into the grass roots, with its local membership, and upwards into the global community, through its connections with DPI.

Its achievements during the decade had been remarkable, for no other disability pressure group had forced society to consider the disabling barriers and negative attitudes that disabled people faced as a denial of their human rights. No other body had managed to identify charity and segregated institutions as part of that process in a way that the 'public' could understand and appreciate. And finally, no other body had managed to make disabled people proud of who they were and feel that their impairments were to be embraced, not denied or eradicated. Such achievements, however, did not minimise the problems that continued to beset and often undermine the organisation, which stemmed from this rapid growth itself.

In this chapter we have concentrated on the organisational and political issues that confronted the BCODP in its first ten years of existence. One of the factors that makes new social movements new, however, and different from other kinds of political organisation, is that as well as building an organisation and achieving political gains, they seek to transform the consciousness of the membership. Richard Wood, current Director of the BCODP, sees the social model as the link between concrete achievements and developing consciousness:

> There was the intensity of uncertainty of people still unsure about just how and if we were going to be able to take on board the broad range of issues that faced us. I think the thing that started to make it clearer was the total acceptance of the social model as being the core of the movement, which it soon became. It was something that people could then adopt and feel a part of.

It is this transformation in the consciousness of disabled people that we will explore in the next chapter.

NOTE

1 Section 64 funding (Section 64 of the Health Services and Public Health Act 1968) is provided by the Secretary of State to assist voluntary organisations in the health and social services field in promoting or providing similar services to the statutory authorities.

Chapter 6

Disability consciousness

The very existence of a social movement indicates that differences exist regarding the meaning of some aspects of reality.

(Benford and Hunt 1995: 85)

INTRODUCTION

This chapter will focus on the way disabled people have redefined the problem of disability as the product of a disabling society rather than individual limitations or loss, despite the fact that the rest of society continues to see disabled people as chance victims of a tragic fate. We will then consider how this process has required the redefinition of self and a recognition that the personal is political. Finally we consider the challenges to negative disability imagery that this personal liberation has produced, and the attempts to develop positive imagery through the newly emerging disability culture. Central to this will be the role of the social model and the recognition of disability as oppression.

It is also worth making the point here that, for us, transforming both personal and social consciousness is one of the key factors that separates new social movements from the old, more traditional social movements. Judy Hunt provides an appropriate definition of consciousness: 'For me, consciousness is the whole change in the way people view themselves and their relationship with the rest of society.'

PERSONAL AND TRAGIC

Transforming personal consciousness implies that there is an existing consciousness to be transformed. Usually for disabled people this is structured by the ideology of personal tragedy theory (Oliver 1990). Elspeth Morrison captures this well: 'About ten years ago I personally had no concept that disability could be seen in anything other than a completely negative and awful, totally tragic kind of way.' Maggie Davis describes how this can be internalised and manifests itself as depression:

> I thought, 'This is it, they're shutting me right out just because I'm disabled.' And I then began to realise that things were not as accessible to disabled people as they were to able-bodied people. I started getting pretty depressed after that because I knew things were going to be pretty hard. I couldn't really see what else I could do at the time. I just went into quite a bit of depression after that because I started realising that I didn't have much hope, there wasn't going to be a job. I had nowhere to go and I just wondered 'Well what sort of future is there at all?'.

DENIAL

One response to this feeling of hopelessness is to deny that there is a problem. Nasa Begum describes how her own self-denial was reinforced by her special school:

> All of us as adolescents question our identities, our bodies and everything else for that matter. But somehow, at my school, no discussion was allowed whatsoever. So you think you've got to pretend that you can do it all. No one actually says, 'Well, actually this is how I feel.' Or, 'How do I deal with this?'. Or, 'Yes I'm disabled, but I'm really proud to be disabled, and sod it if people don't like my body, I like it.'

Despite this, she goes on to suggest that her initial attempted response was assimilation:

> Assimilation was what I bought into, hook, line and sinker. I'm a person first and the fact that I happen to have a disability is irrelevant. I think that was a real hard one because I went to all the special schools and all the warehouses that you can find, because I'd always been with disabled people I was fighting to be recognised as something other than disabled. Although now I think being disabled is part of my identity, when I went to non-disabled college I didn't want to be ghettoised and it was a real fight not to be ghettoised with other disabled people.

Ultimately she found an edited collection of the writings of disabled women (Campling 1981), which helped her to stop denying the reality of her body, her feelings about it and her identity as a disabled woman: '*Images of Ourselves* was important in that I knew there were other women who had thought the same sort of stuff.'

Elspeth Morrison describes her own similar reaction: 'I didn't in any way identify as disabled or want to have anything to do with disabled people other than I used to have this sneaking attraction for working with them.' David Hevey, as someone with a hidden impairment, initially took the opportunity to pass as non-disabled:

> The point about a hidden impairment like epilepsy is that you get an optional passport to the able-bodied land, and most take it in the first instance because that's what social forces tell you to do. You don't have any consciousness to do otherwise. So, I became an epileptic at 15 which led to an entire collapse of my self and my social relations.

BE GRATEFUL AND REASONABLE

The process of transforming consciousness is usually not a cathartic one akin to a religious conversion, but a slow and painful struggle to transform both your view of the world and your own place within it. Phillip Mason describes this painful process:

> Some people felt it was selfish, rather radical, to hit out and kick against everything. You've got to understand that the political clarity that Paul Hunt and UPIAS had developed wasn't necessarily comfortable for many disabled people. Many people felt that we should be grateful recipients of charity. We really were conscious of that, and I'm not putting down my fellow disabled people, because I was one of them. We really felt that actually it was really nice of society to let us in. As individuals, and perhaps even collectively, we were very shy and very retiring and perhaps very self-conscious, not assertive at all.

According to Phillip, overcoming shame was a key factor, and that led to people wanting to appear to be reasonable in their demands:

> One was almost ashamed of oneself. The politicising process is something that's happened during the last ten years, in which I

have come to accept myself as I am. I'm not ashamed of myself as I am but aware perhaps of my intellectual vulnerability. I am also aware of my not wanting to upset people. I think that one of the things that concerned one at the time in the early 1980s was that perhaps the BCODP was rocking the boat a bit. I wasn't aware of that myself but I do know that some disabled people did think that.

Being reasonable was also, as Elsa Beckett explains, not going where one was not wanted:

I can remember back now to incidents that happened before the BCODP which I would never put up with now, like being refused admission to a shop. I can't believe now, looking back, that I just swore at the shop keeper and went on and did nothing more. All right, I wrote to the manager, but never got a reply, never followed it up, never dreamt of going to the papers about it. It was insulting and degrading behaviour but you let it slip past. I think the isolation of being disabled then is the thing that strikes me looking back now. I wouldn't have thought of writing to RADAR about it somehow. I never even thought of contacting any local disability organisation at that time, and I wouldn't have thought of writing to a disability journal and saying 'Do you know this is happening, this is disgusting.' That picture has changed and I wouldn't put up with that sort of discrimination now. Of course I still put up with other discriminations one puts up with. You see these buses sailing past you merrily, don't you? It's quite strange, the levels of conscious action that one reaches.

BEARING WITNESS

One of the key mechanisms through which personal conscious-ness is often transformed is by sharing experiences with other people in similar situations or who face similar problems. Elspeth Morrison explains how this happened to her:

In the early days, if you take the personal as political argument, then meetings were deeply political in that it was very much personal experience which was getting people up and talking; about what it was like to have their particular impairment, what things disabled them, how the world saw them and what it felt to be like that.

However, contact with other disabled people in order to share experience is not always comfortable, as Nasa Begum found out:

> I can remember when I got my first flat, which was in Hampshire. Purely by coincidence, Phillip Mason came to see it, and I was mega-proud of having my first flat, and he said to me, 'Well, this is all right for the time being, but you're never going to want to live here for too long.' It was in a sheltered housing scheme for elderly people and I thought 'This guy's got no idea. He's got no idea. I want to live here all my life.' I often used to think about him afterwards. He was right. You need to move on, but there was no expectation out there that we will move on, that we will ever want to do anything different.

UNDERSTANDING OURSELVES

Central to the process of transforming consciousness is coming to an understanding of ourselves. Sian Vasey describes her own 'thinking period': 'I was unemployed in 1982 through to April 1983, and in that time I remember having quite a cogitation period. I can remember solidifying on things during that period, developing more of an understanding of my situation.' She then describes the point at which she eventually arrived:

> Well, by being a disabled person, I mean a person who has an impairment but who is disabled by society and who has an awareness of the fact that their position in society is not inevitable. This is what I didn't understand in 1980 and I'm sure millions and millions of disabled people don't understand now.

Rachel Hurst describes a similar process, after a cathartic initial realisation:

> In 1975 I experienced a conversion on 'the great road to Damascus' when I realised firstly that I was a disabled person, and secondly and almost instantaneously what discrimination was. I couldn't say that I could articulate it then as I can now but I knew that it was discrimination.

The collective element of that transformation in consciousness is articulated by Phillip Mason:

> The disability movement is the struggle against oppression, against segregation. It's against the victimisation of a minority group because that's what disabled people were. Now I wouldn't have used that language in the early 1980s, or even in the mid-1980s, but the thing about the politicising process is that you actually identify with the language and what it's saying.

When Nasa Begum came to a personal understanding that the problems were not hers but society's, this caused her to withdraw initially rather than seek the support of other disabled people:

> My gut reaction was that it's not my problem. I began to think 'Why should I have to be carried up steps?'. But because everything around me made me feel that 'You're just being an ungrateful git', I began to think 'Well, maybe I am and that life would be a lot easier if I just swallowed it all and said – fine, I'll be carried up steps. I don't mind if I can't get to the library and I do like to spend my adolescence at local shopping centres, shaking cans for money.' I didn't bend, quite surprisingly. I just dropped out of the council for the disabled and activities with disabled people.

FIGHTING BACK

Over the centuries, many individual disabled people have fought against the negative and tragic stereotypes foisted upon them by a dominant culture. One way of fighting back is personal rejection of the dominant disabling culture. Micheline Mason explains:

> Like many disabled people, I have belonged to the disability movement since childhood. The day I threw away the holy water from Lourdes and said to Jesus, 'I think they are missing the point' was the day I joined the movement. I was 9 years old. I did not know if there were any other members then, or if it was just me and Him. Certainly there was no support from surrounding adults, who told me I had very strange ideas. I lived in a world of my own, I was unrealistic, I must learn to face facts.

A second way of fighting back against a disabling culture is to get involved oneself in cultural production, usually through the arts. Disability arts and culture came flooding onto the disability movement's agenda in the mid-1980s, providing a very important channel to promote our newly discovered identity. In 1987 the London Disability Arts Forum (LDAF) was launched with the magazine *DAIL*. Both the organisation and magazine (which, due to overwhelming national demand, had a much wider geographical distribution than intended by the funders) have been fundamental to the development of a cultural expression of our lives. The disability movement from then on was considerably strengthened.

It was Vic Finkelstein, Anne Rae and Sian Vasey who were instrumental in founding the disability arts initiatives. In his presentation at the LDAF launch, Vic clearly demonstrated why a disability culture was largely absent until then:

Firstly, there is a great deal of uncertainty amongst disabled people whether we do want 'our own culture'. After all, we all have had the experiences of resisting being treated as different, as inferior to the rest of society. So why now, when there is much greater awareness of our desire to be fully integrated into society, do we suddenly want to go off at a tangent and start trying to promote our differences, our separate identity? Secondly, at this time, even if we do want to promote our own identity, our own culture, there has been precious little opportunity for us to develop a cultural life. Certainly few of us would regard the endless hours that disabled people used to spend basket weaving under the direction of occupational therapists in day centres as an artistic contribution that disabled people made to the cultural life of humankind.

His hopes for the future were: 'disabled people presenting a clear and unashamed self-identity'. In order to do this he felt it was:

essential for us to create our own public image, based upon free acceptance of our distinctive group identity. Such a cultural identity will play a vital role in helping us develop the confidence necessary for us to create the organisations which we need to promote the social change that we all want. It is vital that all disabled people join together in their own organisation so that there is a creative interaction between disabled people who are involved with the politics of disability and disabled people involved in the arts. It is this interaction which can be particularly fruitful in helping us to take the initiative in developing a new disability culture.

Vic's words of encouragement were hardly needed, for over a hundred disabled people attending the day were already fired up with the notion of radical expression through disability art.

From LDAF came a plethora of comedy, poetry, drama and songs depicting our new-found liberation and presenting our struggle in a form and style that were both challenging and empowering. A roving disabled person's cabaret club, symbolically named 'The Workhouse', was conceived by Geoff Armstrong [a founder member of the disability arts movement], whereby disabled performers were given support and perhaps more importantly an accessible environment from which to perform. Access for disabled spectators was also regarded as important, since so few arts venues provided adequate facilities.

Elspeth Morrison, who has been involved in disability arts almost from the outset, does draw our attention to the fact that being involved in the arts can often bring disabled people difficulties, not least because it is not regarded as proper work:

> The education system, as it works here for disabled and non-disabled children, is that we're encouraged to think of arts practice or cultural practice as something that weirdos, bohemians and pinkies do. The advice, if you say, 'Oh I want to do a job in the arts', is 'Well don't do it. It's not a proper job and you won't make any money.' The latter certainly is true, you won't make any money, but it is a job.

She goes on to suggest that not all disabled artists would see themselves as engaging in alternative cultural production in any case:

> Well all art is, by its very nature, engaging in cultural production, is reflecting something. It's saying something, whether you agree with it or not, it's making some sort of shift in your consciousness. All these people who say, 'Oh I'm just an artist' – well bollocks to them!

And finally, she points out that alternative cultural practice means making wider connections with the disability movement:

If disabled people's organisations are exploring the notion of having a culture and talking about it in a broad sense, not just as an arts thing, then you've got to have some kind of cultural practice that reflects what is going on in the movement.

David Hevey endorses this and goes further:

The problem with the politics of representation is that most people don't know how to get it back to physical struggle, and unfortunately most people in the politics of representation don't want to get it back to physical struggle. Well, physical action is more important, and at the end of the day, you have to nail down representation as the handmaiden of actual physical material struggle.

A third way of fighting back is to engage in political rather than cultural practice. This both is empowering to the individuals who engage in such practice and confronts dominant imagery of disabled people as passive and accepting. Joe Hennessey discusses this in respect of action around the issue of parking for disabled motorists:

I think probably it was because I realised that if I didn't speak then nothing was going to be done. There would be no proper provision made for disabled motorists. I realised that and that it wasn't only me. I could envisage the problems it was going to cause to other people as well. So I said, 'Hey, we've got a right to be here. These are our city centres as well.' This is when we were coming out and being political really for the very first time.

Ken Davis describes the power of political action in hospital:

This night nurse had been terrible and all the patients were moaning and I said, 'Right, if we're going to do something, are you all agreed? Are we going to do something about this or aren't we? If you just moan, nothing will get done.' This nurse was awful and so they said, 'Yeah, we'll do something', and I said, 'Well if you give me your say so I'll go down and speak to Dr W about it, as long as you all back me up.' So they said, 'OK.' I went down to Dr W's office and I was able to say with confidence, 'This nurse behaved in an unacceptable manner and has ill treated this particular patient.' He was very angry with me and he said, 'How dare you come down here like this.' You know, the usual stuff, and he sent me back to the ward.

Anyhow, they summoned the nurse down and she said I was a liar. Then he summoned me back down and said, 'You're a liar, the nurse says so.' And I said, 'No, I'm not a liar, and if you think I am please go and ask the rest of the patients.' So he really couldn't do anything else but then retract what he'd said, and he removed the nurse from the ward.

Phillip Mason suggests that fighting back for some was not an intellectual exercise but an attempt to achieve a better life:

John Evans, Liz Briggs, and other people like that wanted to leave [the home]. It was a very practical thing. It wasn't an intellectual exercise. They just wanted to leave. They wanted a life which they could run for themselves and decide for themselves.

Ann MacFarlane expresses some concern that in transforming personal consciousness, one may be merely swapping one ortho-doxy for another. She describes the necessity of thinking out one's own position for oneself:

It's taken me so long to get to my own process of thinking without just parrot-fashioning what other people have told me. It's like I've taken on the institutionalisation viewpoint for years and years and I've now taken on the politicised viewpoint. Yet all the time I've been trying to do what's right. I think what worries me a little bit is always that fear that I might get it really wrong, and that the radical part of the movement would crush me without giving me a chance to say 'Well OK, I did get it wrong but it isn't that I did it deliberately to see if I could destroy anything or anybody.' And I think that would be really sad.

In reflecting on her own experiences in disability organisations in three countries, Millie Hill suggests that a key difference in the British movement is its concern with personal consciousness. This supports our earlier assertion that the British movement is a new social movement:

I was very much involved in disability associations in the US and Canada, but for me it had a different feel. It wasn't that personal, it was more like a business type of activity. I used to go not because it was something that I felt deep inside, but because I felt it was something I felt I should be doing. To be honest with you I did it mostly for the excitement, because in America we were very much involved in direct action at that time and primarily around issues of trying to make buildings more accessible to people with mobility problems. What I'm trying to say is that it really started to touch me about three or four years ago when it took on a much more personal focus – I became much more aware that these things touched me personally. Before that I was somewhat removed and as I say, I went along primarily for the kick really.

POLITICAL CONSCIOUSNESS

There are many routes to transforming personal into political consciousness. At the core, however, is a rejection of disability as personal tragedy. Maggie Davis describes the first stage in her journey from personal to political consciousness: 'I was beginning to feel that something was dreadfully wrong out there.' For Rachel Hurst, this transformation came as a gradual realisation: 'What I found, after about a year or two I suppose, was that it was absolutely hopeless doing it on your own and that having other disabled people as part of your struggle was absolutely essential.'

For Nasa Begum, who had opted out of disability organisations, it was a television programme that brought her 'in from the cold':

I knew that disabled people were organising and getting it together and doing a lot more than I was. I had seen a programme about America on telly and I remember that it was just the most amazing experience to actually sit there and watch it. It's going to sound really stupid now, but I just never imagined disabled people getting it together and actually regaining control over their lives. But I really saw it as some-thing that happened in America.

For her, the creation of the CIL in Berkeley was like a beacon and, as she explains, her emerging consciousness of disability as a political issue was given further impetus by another television programme:

I used to say, whenever I couldn't get in anywhere, 'It's OK, I'm pissing off to America. I'm going to Berkeley so don't worry.' That was my goal, to go to live in Berkeley, because I thought I'd have a much better time over there. But I think around that time

I also started to see disability as an external issue. There was another programme around at the time, I think it was around killing disabled infants or allowing disabled infants to die at birth. They had this 14-year-old disabled young woman on who said her life was awful, that it was a tragedy and that she wished she'd died. I can remember I wrote to *Radio Times* and complained about it and said it was exactly those sorts of images that were preventing disabled people getting control and actually being able to live positive lives. So although I wouldn't have put a political slant on it at the time, those were some of the things that were influencing me.

And her consciousness took a further step forward when she began to address the interlocking issues of disability and race in a politically active way:

I know what happens with disabled people and with black people if you start saying critical things. It's all the 'chip on your shoulder' stuff and that you are a real militant. That's a kind of a worry. But I didn't come into disability politics, I don't think, as a token representative. I didn't come in on black issues. I came in on my personal experience and perhaps my interest around IL and the burden and gratitude stuff. All that made me much more politically aware. So I guess getting involved in organisations of disabled people is essential. I'm involved with the black disabled people's group too.

For others, it was contact with other disabled people who had already made the journey from personal to political consciousness that was crucial. In Stephen Bradshaw's case, it was contact with Vic Finkelstein:

I'm not saying that I was politically aware because I wasn't. It was only through Vic that I began to be aware of an entirely different way of looking at things. It was rather different from just helping each other. I'd been changing my views because I suppose I was a very middle-class sort of person who happened to become disabled, and was fortunate to be able to carry on relatively successfully as a disabled person because I was an outgoing person, I was the sort of person who could get what I wanted. I was concerned that other people didn't have the advantages that I had; not because I was middle-class necessarily but because I had an ability to get things out of people, and that was very useful to me. I suppose I became more and more political through – politically aware, not political as such – through Vic and chatting with Vic and others about how you actually achieve things more efficiently and more quickly for disabled people. It took me a while to accept that militant action was an option and the techniques of raising the ante and having the structure to raise the ante when things go wrong were important. It was this which Vic demonstrated; how you would operate in terms of collectively getting together and maintaining a position. I've always found that, in a way, difficult. I didn't see that one could become totally extreme and achieve what you're after. But with all the other changes it was clear that in fact by politicising people, by being extreme, you actually began to make progress. It seemed to work by osmosis. People were beginning to adopt, if you like, the BCODP approaches but they would never admit that the BCODP has had any effect on the way they operate, on them as disabled people, or on their organisations trying to help disabled people.

Richard Wood had a similar experience, but at a later time and with Ken Davis as the key influence:

I was a late arriver on the scene, I'm afraid. I appeared on the scene in 1985 when I moved to Derbyshire and, along with other people, helped set up a CIL. I did a lot of work with people like Ken, who's probably been the biggest influence on my life in terms of disability politics. I was like many disabled people who knew there were issues, who knew there were discriminations and prejudices, who felt very angry about them, but actually had not discovered the literature that defined them and had not discovered any forum in which to project them. And I still find that today. There are still people banging on the table when you're talking about a social model as though they've never heard of it before. The social model was an immense liberation to me.

The social model was introduced to David Hevey by Elspeth Morrison: 'I met Elspeth, God rest her soul, at some political thing. That whole thing, the medical model and the social model, it was so simple and brilliant.'

For Alan Holdsworth, national organiser of DAN, it was a non-disabled woman called Izzie who forced him to confront the issue

of disability and helped him to make sense of his gradually
emerging consciousness:

> Most of my life has been spent in denial of myself as a disabled
> person. What forced me to confront that was a non-disabled
> woman called Izzie, who was politically active in lots of other
> campaigns. She was one of these people who would just not let
> you off the hook. I ended up working with people with learning
> difficulties in Chesterfield and in total isolation from the
> movement, but the conclusions I was reaching there in the
> end made me write a song called 'Choices and Rights' which
> the movement haven't amended since. So I must have been
> getting some perceptions right even in isolation. I joined the
> DCDP particularly to try and get them to take on board people
> with learning difficulties' issues and to bring people with
> learning difficulties into it. At the same time people began to
> hear 'Choices and Rights' and started booking me for gigs.

The transformation of disability consciousness from being a
personal to a political issue was not always a journey from the
apolitical to the political. For some it was a matter of transferring
an existing political consciousness into the arena of disability
issues. Jenny Morris describes her own experience:

> I'd been political since I was 16 in terms of being involved in
> trade union politics and the Labour Party. It just came naturally.
> I didn't think about deliberately doing it. A friend of mine who
> co-ordinated all the support that was given to me while I was
> still in hospital was also very active in the Labour Party and is
> one of my closest friends; she said to me within days of my
> accident that if ever there was an exciting time to be disabled,
> now is it. Although I wasn't properly aware of disability as an
> issue, it was around, and so non-disabled people in the Labour
> Party knew that it was a political issue. So my friend, Jane, could
> say to me that now is an exciting time to be disabled, because
> disabled people are actually organising as disabled people.

Her involvement in the politics of disability was more than an
intellectual exercise even while she was in hospital. She further
explains:

> The way I felt about it was very much tied up with the conflict
> that I was experiencing within Stoke Mandeville because, as a

political person, I immediately came into conflict with the hierarchy. I remember that I was the last person admitted to the old spinal unit before they moved into the new one, and they moved just three weeks after my accident. There was an article in the *Guardian* by Ann Shearer about the opening of the new unit, but she was also criticising Stoke for focusing so much on male competitiveness and the 'stiff upper lip', with no counselling. The phrase – no counselling – stood for all sorts of things, like no explanation of the personal experience, no room for sharing what you're going through or getting help with that. It was all about physical achievement and competitiveness. I wrote a letter in response to that article saying that I agreed. There was no counselling, and I described what had happened to me, and I asked for anybody who had a similar experience to write to me. Thinking about it, it was a real cheek on my part because I'd only been there three weeks and I wasn't even out of bed. I'd got another five weeks to go before I got into a wheelchair. None the less I got hundreds of letters and phone calls. It was wonderful. I've got a file upstairs full of all these letters. The first phone call I got was that evening, the day the letter appeared in the *Guardian*, from this woman who had been spinal-cord injured some years ago and who had two children. My own daughter was just over a year old at that point, so I was wanting to get into contact with other women who had been in a similar situation. We had a two-hour telephone conversation. I suppose exploring the personal was always tied up with the political for me. It had been before and it was afterwards.

Mike Barrett cut his political teeth in the trade union movement. This stood him in good stead when he moved into disability politics, and he already had an understanding about some of the ways organisations operated:

I then moved to London, and I think that was when I started to understand what politics was about, I used to go to the meetings there very regularly. I'd become a shop steward and used to enjoy having battles with the boss, realising that there was quite a bit more you could get away with when you were a shop steward instead of just an ordinary worker. We had communists running our branch at that time, and there was a tendency that they would change the resolutions a little bit to suit a communist approach to it more than ours.

Vic Finkelstein had come from a different political background altogether. Having actively fought against apartheid in South Africa, been imprisoned and then deported, he explains what this involvement enabled him to bring to disability politics in Britain:

I think it's quite important in a way because I came to the disability movement through a political movement – not the other way round. The strength, the greatest support that I had in terms of developing social protest in disability, was gained from my earlier political background. There were able-bodied individuals, not in the disability movement at all, who were able to recognise and support some of the things that we had been doing, and they helped to clarify some of these things. Some of them encouraged me to get involved in disability organisations and to bring to them political interpretations. So some of the arguments that I was raising about oppression of disabled people originated from oppression of black people. It was a direct connection.

DEAF CONSCIOUSNESS AND DISABILITY CULTURE

It would not be appropriate to leave this chapter, which discusses consciousness and culture, without some discussions of deaf consciousness and culture. Paddy Ladd proudly affirms what this is and how it was, and is, produced:

Culture as in art is one thing. Culture as in deaf culture is another. Basically deaf people whose first language is BSL [British Sign Language] should be seen as a linguistic minority. It helps if you think of us as parallel to, say, an Asian community. Deaf people have been joyfully getting together since time began, and our schools go back to the 1790s and our clubs to the 1820s. Our language is much older. Deaf people marry each other 90 per cent of the time, 10 per cent have deaf children. Our customs and traditions have been passed down the ages and these, together with our values and beliefs, constitute our culture. These parallel other linguistic minorities. The whole definition of culture is so much wider than the one the disability movement is espousing.

He also makes an impassioned plea for the continued existence of their own schools as a way of maintaining deaf identity and consciousness, pointing out that this remains a bone of contention between NUD and the (rest of the) disability movement:

And the centrepiece of it is our schools. All this has been achieved despite the disgusting work of oralists, our schools are where we are socialised into the culture. Integration threatens to destroy these centres of achievement, quite apart from the damage caused by thrusting lone deaf kids into mainstream schools with no access to what teachers are saying, no easy access to the rest of the school's activities, no deaf adults, the total lack of a peer group, etc., etc. The irony is that 80 per cent of deaf kids are integrated, with no little thanks to disabled people; we are the ones sent into the Valley of Undeaf, not they.

This attempt to see themselves as a 'linguistic minority' rather than as disabled people has raised some political dilemmas and conflicts, as he goes on to explain:

When it came to the Waring [anti-discrimination] Bill, the NUD let each member decide what they wanted to do. Some decided to join in with the BDA's [British Deaf Association's] first massive lobby of Parliament, which was held in conjunction with other disabled people, although deaf people formed the great majority of the lobby, despite what some disabled people now say. They decided to join in because (1) they realised that the government were always going to classify deaf people under disabled for the foreseeable future, and thus the only political solution for now could be found there; (2) they realised that such a lobby would be a magnificent confidence booster for deaf people, both as individuals and in getting a taste of their collective power. Those who opposed it noted that this first ever mass lobby arranged by the BDA should have been on a deaf issue, particularly the education issue. They also found the 'shepherding' of deaf people almost unthinkingly to this lobby too close in style to the old missioners'/welfare officers' approach, of an elite making the decisions and directing people unquestioningly into it.

SIGNIFICANT VICTORIES

In talking about the subjective dimensions of life, it is difficult to be concrete about successes. However, John Evans is certain about our success at both the personal and the political level:

> One of the successes is the pride disabled people find in their organisation. I think that's a great success as well as our sense of identity, our sense of meaning in life. These are the important things to me because that's what disabled people's lives are about. It's not living in isolation. It's not just struggle and being against the system and fighting the system. While we have to do a lot of this, it's also about actually creating a positive identity for us as people and positive images in society at large. It's had its impact and hopefully we'll see disabled people reading the news and so on before long.

These personal victories, according to John, are significant because they have brought about political and social change:

> There was no question that it wasn't political. Most of us felt that what we were involved with was political change. We also wanted to see social change in society at large and in our local communities and throughout the country. Because what we were endeavouring to do was to develop pioneering schemes, it had to fit into a social strategy. That wasn't going to be easy, so we realised we had to change society in a small way but in an important way. It was going to have a lot of wider implications in the future. We were political. I think part of the process of IL and how you go about it politicises people. It makes people more politically aware because they gain knowledge about what they are doing, they gain knowledge about the system and how the system works, and to a certain extent we were able to manipulate the system or even work the system to our own advantage.

People First make similar points in terms of two notable successes they have had: the acceptance of the term 'learning difficulties' and the enforced U-turn by the Charity Commissioners to enable them to register as a charity. Initially the Charity Commission had refused to allow people with learning difficulties to become trustees, as it was deemed their impairment rendered them incapable. People First mounted a highly successful campaign drawing in the support of lawyers, communicating through the popular media, rallying the support of other disabled people's organisations and generally lobbying all sectors of society. Their power and strength can be marked by the repeal of the age-old charity law which prohibited the 'mentally incapacitated' from the responsibilities of trusteeship. They are rightly proud of these achievements:

> What makes me feel strong? Well one thing that makes me feel strong was the changing of the label 'mental handicap' to 'people with learning difficulties'. That made me feel real powerful. Another thing is the Charity Commission. We've just now become a charity for people with learning difficulties.

FURTHER ROADS TO TRAVEL?

There is still much to do, of course. As well as the millions of disabled people all over the world who still lack political consciousness in terms of disability issues, there are also issues about how to turn developing consciousness into a social movement, as Sian Vasey reminds us:

> I would just say that this might explain why the women's movement seems to be defunct, in real terms. While there's a huge feminist consciousness around, a feminist consciousness doesn't make a movement, or a disability consciousness doesn't make a movement.

Elspeth Morrison makes the point that the arts movement can make a contribution to involving people in disability politics:

> I believe that the arts movement can do more and has done a lot in getting people, who the BCODP otherwise might have difficulty attracting, involved in the idea of being a disabled person and in the movement more generally.

CONCLUSIONS

In this chapter we have concentrated on what, in our view, constitutes the most significant issue that makes new social movements different from other kinds of movement; namely that of transforming the individual and collective consciousness of the membership. We are not suggesting that this journey of transformation is complete. Indeed, as we have implied, it has only just begun, but having begun, it is impossible to return to the start of the journey.

Again, Richard Wood provides an appropriate summary of where we are, looking both backwards and forwards:

> The definition of issues and the identity of ourselves as people distinct in society, in a unique position in society, has got to be the key success. I don't know if other people would agree with that or not. Without that self-identification I think we would still be struggling. We'd not only be struggling on trying to define terms and identify issues, but we'd be struggling in terms of our confidence and our ability to address them. Discovering our identity as disabled people is very, very important. It's still important today, otherwise people won't value themselves. I think that is probably the biggest success that the movement has been able to point to. It is our movement, nobody else owns it. We know who we are. I think we're fairly clear about where we're going and why we're going there.

Just where the next steps of the journey will take us will be discussed in the following chapter.

Chapter 7

Making connections through rights and empowerment

> The present prominence of identity politics is linked to an increasing recognition that social theory itself must be a discourse with many voices, not a monological speaking of a simple and unitary truth or its successive approximations.
>
> (Calhoun 1994: 4)

INTRODUCTION

This chapter will attempt to widen the discussion to look at the connections between a whole variety of oppressed groups and at the tactics for achieving human rights, notably through the process of empowerment at individual and collective levels. Political demands like these have profound implications for the political process, and these will be considered in the light of theories of new social movements.

Despite the seminal work begun by UPIAS in linking disability to oppression, the theoretical work linking disability to other forms of oppression has yet to be done in a systematic way. Apart from the article published by Abberley (1987) and more recent work by Stuart (1992) and Morris (1991, 1992), there has been almost no collaborative work to establish a coherent, collective basis for understanding and attacking simultaneous oppression, although some work looking at the experience of simultaneous oppression has now been undertaken (Zarb and Oliver 1993; Begum et al. 1994). This lack is, again, partly a resource problem. If you are struggling simply to survive, then intellectualising is the last activity that may seem relevant. What follows is part description, part analysis of how some of these issues have none the less begun to impact on the movement.

Thus, as the epigraph to this chapter implies, the movement will need to find a way of speaking about disability issues which includes everyone and does not result in disunity and in-fighting within the movement. As David Hevey trenchantly puts it: 'I am pro much of the whole identity politics thing, so long as it results in Jerusalem, not in some side issue.'

DISABILITY, OUR HISTORY AND OPPRESSION

Judy Hunt locates the emergence of these issues historically and in the wider society:

Probably what was happening to black people was the most powerful link, and people were beginning to make those connections. The women's movement came a bit later, towards the end of the 1960s, and then there was also the student movement at around the same time. So there was a sort of general fervour going on, and this, coupled with liberalising ideas about institutions in general, the questioning of what happened to people in institutions, led to connections being made, though it's difficult to specify how. Then a bit later the link between mental handicap [learning difficulties] and getting people out of hospitals and institutions arose as a movement. You could also see the beginning of international developments – different people in different countries looking at the same sorts of issues. In Australia, for example, people were writing about the limitations of institutions, rights to rehabilitation and to some extent about discrimination. I think people began to talk about oppression a little bit.

Micheline Mason draws attention to our lack of understanding of the concept of internalised oppression and her perceptions of the ways this has kept the disability movement divided:

The effects of internalised oppression have not been well understood by the main body of the disability movement. There are still great divisions between us, now being acknowledged as the whiteness and maleness and middle-classness of its membership become more and more embarrassing. Young disabled people are still unrepresented, and people with learning difficulties feel greatly marginalised within the movement. The deaf community's ambivalent position on identity as disabled people is just another facet of internalised oppression.

Rachel Hurst, on the other hand, suggests that her experiences of sexism made a significant contribution to her later understanding of disablism:

I think being a woman and realising the hell of being a woman in a male society has perhaps made it easier for me to see what's happening. The added bit of being a disabled person and seeing actually what's happening to people like us was therefore easier.

Nasa Begum, following Stuart (1992), calls this simultaneous oppression:

Many of us will experience simultaneous oppression. Many of us will identify with different bits of our identity at different times. Different issues become important. Although none of them can you ever leave on the doorstep and say, 'It's irrelevant.' But sometimes, for example, the appalling treatment you get in a hospital; a lot of it is around being disabled but some of it is this sexist crap that they come out with in terms of us as women. Do you know what I mean? Lots of people say to me that black disabled people identify disability as the main issue, which worries me, because we shouldn't be trying to get people to separate our identity. But the reality is that some of us, at different stages of our lives, are going to identify with different things as at that particular point being more pressing, perhaps.

DISABILITY, SIMULTANEOUS OPPRESSION AND THE MOVEMENT

Stephen Bradshaw, who was one of the original Council members of the BCODP, describes the dilemma faced by that Council:

We made considerable efforts to get the Asian blind and disabled group involved. We went to particular efforts. We had no money, we sent out letters and made phone calls, we discussed things with them, we tried. So we actually made quite an effort, but nothing came of it. So I think it's a difficult one that because, while it's absolutely right that more should have been done, we could have spent an awful lot of time sorting out our relationship with our own 'minority groups'. We would have felt great, and we would have done good works there and formed a sort of unified base which was not sexist, which was not racist etc., but would we have done anything else? That's the only problem I would have with it.

He goes on to point out that no decision was made to exclude particular groups or people, and including people just because of race or gender would have led to charges of tokenism:

We didn't actually make a conscious decision saying, 'Can we do this? Have we the energy? Is this the highest priority at the moment?'. If we were going to start having token people – you know, you've got to have somebody of this race or this colour or you've got to have a woman here, and you begin to have supernumeraries or token positions purely to have somebody upfront. I know it's a very important way forward, and that if you don't make a start, you're not going to get anywhere and change things.

He concludes by stressing that the original priority was 'that we get going and sort the BCODP out in terms of "out there" rather than get our own house in order perfectly'. And he goes on to stress that all political movements inevitably have their internal divisions:

There is always going to be a particular group who's going to have a shout at us. Just as we couldn't sort out matters with the Liberation Network, so they sought separate status with DPI because they didn't agree with the BCODP approach.

Elsa Beckett, another original Council member, makes a similar point and brings it up to date by pointing to the same sorts of difficulty still being faced by local disability organisations:

It is something that will have to be followed up. This time it's coming from the grass roots, isn't it, around the lack of involvement by people from the ethnic minorities. That's something we never addressed at the beginning. I think we were just so concerned about actually getting the BCODP launched, getting money, getting our voice heard, that the whole thing about equal opportunities didn't really get going. But it wasn't taking place at grass roots either. Here in Newham,

40 per cent of the borough come from various ethnic minority groups, and we're still struggling in the various disability organisations that are kind of, I suppose you'd say, mainstream organisations, not specifically concerned with Asian or black people or helping them to get a fair representation. We haven't got anything like that. I'm on the committee on Action and Rights for People with Disabilities, and we haven't got one single black representative on that yet. And it's the same with the Newham Association for the Disabled; there's just one representative from the Asian elders. At the grass roots, it's an ongoing thing, but we've got to get better representation in our local organisations and then hopefully that will feed up into the BCODP.

It is also important to remember, that in the early years, there was not such a great awareness of the issues surrounding other oppressions. Millie Hill makes the point about her own recently emerging awareness of their interconnectedness:

My politicisation around disability issues began three to four years ago. I'd already been very politicised around the issues of race because I'd come from a very political background in the US and Canada, where I was very much involved in demonstrations and pressure groups and support groups who dealt with issues of racism, but not so much around issues of disability. Until I came to Britain, and even then it didn't start immediately, because I've been here about six years. But my politicisation around disability came about three years ago, primarily as a consequence of being associated with disability organisations and other disabled individuals. I'd lived previously in an academic atmosphere, but it was after I left law school and started to become affiliated with disability organisations that my political awareness around disability issues was much more heightened. Prior to that I was political but not in the sense of disability awareness.

Nasa Begum recognises the need to build a collective movement which is given coherence by developing an appropriate theoretical framework, but points to some of the difficulties of ensuring that this connects to individual experience:

It's very important that we work as a collective, that disabled people get together and start organising and develop a political perspective. But one of the things that has perhaps put me off was that, while I recognise the need for a theoretical academic framework, I feel as though it's gone so much down that line that it's actually left a lot of people behind, and to me it's in danger of becoming a movement that will represent an elite few. Despite saying that, I do think it's really important and we've got to push it and got to develop much more. But, for example, for me as a black disabled woman it doesn't acknowledge a lot of my experiences. It doesn't give me much to relate to. I find it very interesting that I've only become politically aware of being black in the last two years, and that's like at the age of 27. What was I doing?

And she goes on to describe the pain that this emerging awareness can cause:

I'm constantly using the quote of Martin Luther King – 'To be black and to be conscious is to be angry for the rest of your life.' I think you can use that same quote – 'To be disabled and to be conscious . . . .' For many of us, just carrying on with being black and being disabled and being a woman and all that is not only to be angry. Sometimes people end up getting quite hurt or quite confused, because it does mean you have to deal with your family where you could have to deal with some difficult dynamics, and you have to deal with your friends.

A positive departure from making some of the 'conscious connections' that Nasa referred to has been well articulated by the lesbian and gay communities within the disability movement. Two leading activists, Kath Gillespie-Sells and David Ruebain, wrote a booklet and participated in a Channel 4 documentary which highlighted the parallels between lesbians and gays and disabled people 'coming out':

When lesbians and gay men come out, they declare to the world and themselves that they embrace their sexuality and all the joy and pain and ability to love that this brings. They begin to reject the guilt, the shame, the self hatred and the abuse and to become at peace with themselves. Surprising as it may seem, this experience can be almost exactly the same when disabled people come out and declare they are disabled. Moreover, when we come out as disabled people to lesbians and gay men, we can help them in their journeys and, of course, vice versa. When we tear down barriers that separate one of us, we tear down barriers that separate all of us.

(Gillespie-Sells and Ruebain 1992: 213)

Whilst not denying the 'complex struggle' that disabled people from more than one oppressed group face, within and out of the movement, it is important to demonstrate the liberating lessons that have been shared and built upon.

Alan Holdsworth, while fully supporting these moves to include everyone, urges the movement not to forget those disabled people left on what he refers to as 'the plantations': the day centres and residential care:

There's a lot of discussion around including the groups which have a high political connotation, but we don't talk about linking people who are in day centres to the movement; we don't talk about linking people in residential care. What's missing is a sense of our links with the plantations, if you like. Are we still linked with plantations? When we talk about including everybody we go off on the equal ops line, which is fine; no one is disagreeing with that; but the equal ops line surely has got to include people who are in residential care. Surely we can see the problems with that and that we have to address them? Just as, for example, we have to address the inclusion of black people as a separate issue to get black people into the movement, we have to do the same for people in residential care and day centres.

BUILDING A BROAD BASE?

There is also a tactical issue involved as far as the movement is concerned: should it concentrate on solely disability issues or should it consider others, with the potential for divisiveness that may have? This is, of course, an issue that has faced other social movements as well. In feminism, for example, there are major debates about whether women should organise around 'affinities of interest' or on the basis of a common identity.

David Hevey makes a similar point in respect of social movements in general and the gay movement in particular. This analysis leads him to issue a warning to the disability movement:

What happens to movements is that they face their own

powerlessness sometimes and implode. I think that's what happened in the gay movement in the early 1980s, and I was in those arguments. They become a bit like the family where people rip each other apart. If we're not careful we will see the scale of the problem amongst ourselves.

Earlier in our history, disabled people became divided, categorised and controlled on the basis of our individual impairments. As a consequence, there is a reluctance on the part of some disabled people to open the movement to other, potentially divisive issues. As far as the BCODP is concerned, there has never been a policy to focus only narrowly on disability issues and to ignore racism, sexism, ageism and homophobia, but there is no doubt that internal debates have taken place. Millie Hill describes her own experience:

> I got fed up to the back teeth of being told by white disabled people that as black disabled people we shouldn't be concerned with issues of race and disability; that we should be concerned only with issues of disability because that was the fight; that was the most important element in our character. I am of the belief that black disabled people share a lot in common with white disabled people. We have lots of issues in common, but we cannot ignore the fact that to a very large extent there still is that added element of racism that we have to encounter as black people. I didn't think that the white disability movement was taking that on board.

There is also a leadership issue. Patricia Rock criticises the BCODP because of the inadequate representation of minority groups within its management structure:

> It needs to improve on the equal opportunities issues, I must admit that's where I feel strongest. I don't think it's taken on board racism in terms of actually trying to outreach and make sure people from different cultures and backgrounds come onto the management structure of the BCODP. There's no point just saying, 'We've got five black people here today.' You actually need them as part of the political process, you need them part of the executive structure, and that's not there yet. So I feel there's more work needs to be done about that.

Millie Hill makes a similar point in respect of the disability movement in general rather than narrowly of the BCODP:

> One of my primary concerns is still trying to reach black disabled people, and whereas the white disability movement really is moving full steam ahead, I still see very few black people actively involved in that movement. A lot of that is historical because of the way the organisations have been built up. They have been led primarily by white people, white males mostly, and black disabled people are not automatically involved in them.

Whether this constitutes racism within the movement is an emotive question. As far as we are aware there is no evidence to suggest that disabled people are more or less racist than the rest of the population, and as racism is endemic to society, there is no reason to suppose that it will not manifest itself in the organisations which develop in that society. However, the other side of the story relates back to the need to develop awareness and consciousness amongst black disabled people themselves. Nasa Begum makes this point:

> I guess I just ignored the fact that I was black. It's very easy to do it for black disabled people because other people only concentrate on your disability. It's your disability that gets you sent to Treloars. In fact I got put in a lower class because English was my second language. It never occurred to me that this might be racism.

And as she goes on to say, this leads to a reluctance to take up leadership roles or positions in disability organisations. Nasa remains suspicious of being used as a token:

> Ages ago I was asked to be on the management committee of Asian People with Disabilities Alliance, and I said no. Ever since I went to Waltham Forest they've asked me to be on the management committee. At first I was able to refuse because I was involved in doing the research around black disabled people and I felt that, as a council officer, I might have a conflict of interest. But then when I eventually finished my excuses ran out, so I agreed to be a co-optee. But I'm not actually that keen on doing that. I don't know why. I do think it's important that organisations have got to meet and everything, but there's

actually no fun in it. Recently I've started to get to know more disabled people socially, and politics comes out in that obviously, and it's an important part of it. That's the important way round too. On the other hand I could sit on lots and lots of committees as a token black person.

Mike Barrett suggests that the image that the BCODP has of being dominated by people in wheelchairs is, at least in part, the responsibility of other disabled people:

They still only see it as the wheelchair brigade. Well I say, 'That's our fault, we're not prominent enough at the BCODP. We've not put any membership into its regionalisation programme, which we should do. We've got area councils of our own who could affiliate as regional areas and move in. We could take the BCODP over tomorrow, because we would be entitled to affiliate fifty-two branches, but I advise you not to because that's not the way forward. What we've got to do is to ensure that all disabilities are accounted for.' Now I remember in the early days we had a battle royal about who should represent mentally handicapped and mentally ill people. We never used the new terminology then, it was 'mentally handicapped' or 'mentally ill', and I remember the battle over that.

People First, who were centrally involved in struggles to change the term 'mental handicap', forcefully put the opposite point of view: 'I think the BCODP should be more aware of what People First is doing.'

Finally, Nasa Begum points out that the movement must risk fragmentation in order to include everybody's different experiences of disability and to advance further our theoretical understanding:

As black disabled people we have specific experiences. Unless we actually acknowledge those differences and work with them, we're going to leave lots and lots of disabled people out, or it's going to be a movement and a theoretical framework that doesn't really address lots of people's reality.

It is true also that minority groups are now beginning to emerge within the movement. Recent developments in respect of addressing the issue of homophobia are a good example of this. Patricia Rock suggests:

REGARD, of course, being the only organisation campaigning around lesbian and gay issues for people with disabilities, has got a lot to say. Its politics are very, very clear, and I think it could do a lot to facilitate within the BCODP, looking at what are the real issues around heterosexism, how to fight it and how to run training sessions. We ought to think more about training people within the BCODP generally, around how do you look at these things, we need some ongoing running workshops.

While Elsa Beckett is supportive of this, she does return to the issue of resource constraints:

It's very difficult, isn't it? I imagine the workers are very hard pressed doing what they're doing, and I think it's rather too easy to say from outside, 'We should have done this, we should be doing that.' Most disability organisations are really hard pressed to keep afloat. We could say we should have taken up much more over the problems around disabled women's lives, around the ethnic minorities, around lesbians and gays, but I think the difficulty is again that you haven't got enough grassroots groups to work with. For instance, now there are only two small groups of gay men with disabilities organised. Quite what they're doing, how political they are, I don't know. There's GEMMA and REGARD now, there was LANGUID – I don't know if they're still going on, I think not. They're in abeyance at the moment. Also the whole issue around people with learning difficulties.

She goes on to reflect on whether, in the early stages, things could have been done differently, but recognises that these issues seem clearer in hindsight:

Maybe we didn't make it seem accessible enough. Maybe we should have done more outreach work. I don't know if reserving specific places on the council would have worked. Perhaps right at the beginning if we'd said, 'We're not just going to be this group; we've got these spaces and we're looking for them to be filled.' Maybe that would have helped initially. I think the whole thing was so new to some of us that it wouldn't have occurred anyway.

Micheline Mason makes it clear both that the movement needs to change and precisely what changes are necessary:

This will not change until we change our behaviour towards one another quite drastically. No more gossiping about each other's shortcomings. No more ignoring the content of what people are trying to say whilst criticising the language used, no more speaking out against each other in public, no more denying that there is a nasty hierarchy at work, but instead always giving platforms to people 'lower down' to communicate their ideas; no more leaping on each other's mistakes. More than this, it means daring to care for each other, and to show it: writing the appreciative note; thanking each other for our individual contributions; noticing when someone has made a personal breakthrough; allowing each other to rest without guilt; listening during each other's difficult times; remembering that isolation can only be interrupted by one-to-one relationships. It does not mean never disagreeing with anyone, or sharing a different viewpoint, but there are respectful and disrespectful ways of doing this. If we can create this kind of 'nurturing' atmosphere then we can begin to heal these divisions and build a much broader-based movement.

THE RESPONSE OF THE BCODP

These are weighty issues, which confront the disability movement as a whole, and the ways they are addressed will be crucial to its future. As we have suggested, the movement itself is broader than the BCODP, but John Evans outlines his perception of the position of the BCODP in respect of the issues we have been discussing:

I'd like to see lots of Asian groups, lots of black Caribbean groups, all the other ethnic minority groups that are there, that are in existence but don't identify with the British disability movement, as they still see it as white and middle-class and all the rest of it. It's breaking down those barriers that will definitely strengthen the BCODP. We've seen in the last year or so a number of Asian groups now joining us, and black disability groups – it's happening at a very slow scale. It's only a few organisations, but I think those organisations can help bring in others as a result of their joining – when the suspicion and the distrust and all the negative aspects that those groups have of the BCODP as a white middle-class movement start getting disbanded, and they will really put forward our case very strongly. The BCODP should prosper from that and it's an avenue that we have got to go down. We're moving forward a little bit with people with learning difficulties, but people with mental health problems, mental health survivors, are an area of great concern. Why those groups are being marginalised – we're not doing it consciously but there still is that process happening. It's breaking down those barriers. The disability movement in this country is still young and we've still got a lot to learn, much as we've learnt a lot over the last ten years.

Richard Wood also points out that the BCODP is still a very young organisation:

You might say we should have tackled the issues of black disabled people before now, or lesbian and gay disabled people before now, but we are a very, very young movement. The BCODP is in its twelfth year, but I don't think we're in the twelfth year at all. We're probably in our sixth or seventh year. I think we spent the first five years shouting at each other and discovering each other, and working out all those problems of being in a strange environment with a strange new set of politics and philosophies, and just trying to understand what the hell it was that we were trying to say.

He goes on to suggest that in terms of tackling, if not resolving, these issues, the BCODP's record is good:

My own subjective view of all this is that I think the disabled people's movement has been the most open movement in terms of trying to at least understand and address a range of wider issues that impinge on disabled people. I've not seen that to the same degree in other movements. I don't know why that is. I've heard the argument from black people which goes, 'Well, you can't begin to address disability issues within the black movement until the racist issues are solved. Therefore there is no issue for us to prioritise other than that of racism.' Who am I to say, 'You've got it wrong, pal'? I just stand back and say, 'Fine.' However, I do still feel within that sort of framework the question should be asked of disabled people in the black community, 'Do you agree?'. That is the important issue.

Finally he points to some of the steps that are being taken:

Black people, lesbian and gay people, and now the early

formation of a women's group within the BCODP are beginning to answer these questions for themselves; that there is still
an issue, and that issue is still around the oppression of disabled
people, and that's why these groups need to work within our
movement. We will work to eradicate racism, sexism, homophobia and everything else as much as we can within the
movement, but we are a movement that's here to address
primarily disability issues. That is where our first focus
should be.

As one of us has argued elsewhere (Oliver 1995: Ch. 10), the
issue is not whether the disability movement has eradicated all of
the oppressions of capitalism from within it, but whether it
recognises these as issues and is struggling against them. In the
final section of this chapter, we will look at the key issues which
unite, rather than divide, the movement.

WORKING TOGETHER FOR ADL AND CIVIL RIGHTS

While the demands of disabled people for protection against
discrimination go back to the 1970s at least, and received a boost
through the publication of the CORAD (Committee on Restrictions Against Disabled People) Report in 1981, it was not until the
mid-1980s that the movement began to agitate for ADL. In 1989,
the BCODP made a formal commitment to it, and subsequently
the demand was broadened out and there was a commitment to
comprehensive and enforceable civil rights legislation.

As one commentator has pointed out, one of the characteristics
of many new social movements is their demands for civil rights:

> Furthermore, some aspects of new social movement ideology
> are quite clearly concerned with existing political institutions,
> and can very well be understood in terms of citizenship,
> representation and so on. This is especially so with regard to
> a second class of new social movement aims, namely, those
> concerned with 'citizens' rights', that is, with acquiring for
> some section of the population those rights which are ascribed
> to the average citizen, and from which particular groups are
> systematically excluded.
>
> (Scott 1990: 23)

Despite the tensions within the movement discussed above –

and we should say at this point that we regard these tensions as an indication of the strength and not the weakness of the movement – the recently emerging civil rights issue has served to unite different groups. Ann MacFarlane puts it this way:

> The whole political thrust of the movement is moving forward for ADL, for human rights, for civil rights and for all those things in our lives that we really need and all the ways in which people, disabled people, are trying to work together.

And Millie Hill agrees:

> One of the major things I would like to see is ADL. I think it's paramount; not that I believe it's going to solve all our problems overnight, but I think it's going be the way forward for the liberation of disabled people.

Jenny Morris makes the point that the attempts of the disability movement to achieve civil rights for disabled people have been crucial in linking the personal and political; in spelling out the agenda for social change as well as changing the self-identity of disabled people:

> I think it is the most exciting civil rights movement. I think that the challenge that it makes to the rest of society is absolutely fundamental. I just think it's extraordinary the changes that it's trying to bring about. The whole way that people think about themselves and about their impairment. These things are very, very significant and they are about changing society very fundamentally. I think it's very, very difficult but I don't see it going away and it is making the movement stronger. What I have hope for personally is winning the battle about ideas because that's the level on which I'm now operating. In the short term there's not much room for optimism, but I think there's huge potential for changing the way that people think. That would then make a major difference to the lives of individual disabled people. I suppose that's what my hope would be.

David Hevey points out that there are some difficulties in going down the civil rights road:

> The BCODP has a difficult act juggling all the balls in terms of its commitment to civil rights, to which they're slightly

uncritical. For example, many of the charities now support civil rights, and I don't see anyone doing any critical work on why. My theory is because if they get rights then services will grow and they'll gain. That's basically why they support rights. There seems to be a kind of naivety latent within disabled people still; a lot of crips can't get their head round the historical forces ranged against them, and that sometimes errs into a dangerous naivety.

CONCLUSIONS: AFTER ADL?

While recognising the dangers, it seems to us that such legislation is inevitable, and not just in the watered-down version placed on the statute books by the current government in the summer of 1995. But we have to recognise it is a means not an end; it will not guarantee for all disabled people an end to every act of discrimination, let alone ensure our complete inclusion into society. Statutory rights and the judicial process will guarantee neither an end to discrimination nor an inclusive society.

Further, we must guard against the after-effects of success. In the US, according to Scotch (1984), the American movement put so much effort into getting Section 504 of the Rehabilitation Act 1973 signed, incorporating anti-discrimination initiatives into the public sector, that the movement virtually fell apart afterwards, as it had achieved its main goal. Joe Hennessey warns:

> I think this single-minded approach to it is absolutely necessary and it will win the day. There's no doubt about that. What we're talking about is whether it's now, or in five years or whatever. It is going to happen, and once it's happened then the disability movement has got to make sure that, having achieved the legislation, it works and people do have these rights, because it's still going to take a hell of an effort to get equal rights – to get them actually implemented, not just on the statute book.

He goes on to point out the ideological value that such legislation will bring:

> Then we will have a fair society where the worth of disabled people will be recognised and where they will truly have the same opportunities as other people. Twenty years ago that

would have been utopia, now it's still some way off but it's within sight certainly.

Some of the difficulties facing the movement now and into the future have been discussed in this chapter, and we have ended on the optimistic note that the vision of a fairer and more equitable society for disabled people is now a realisable goal and not merely a utopian vision. In the next chapter we will begin to describe some of the dimensions of this new society and to assess its achievability.

Chapter 8

New visions or the existing order?

> Social movements would be of very little significance if they did not call into question not only particular phenomena but a general representation of social life.
>
> (Touraine 1995: 378)

INTRODUCTION

This chapter will look at the implications for society of committing itself to a non-disabling vision of the world. Disabled people over the past twenty years have produced an impressive body of work identifying what needs to be done to create a fairer society for them. Millie Hill comes close to summarising what some of these things might be:

> I would like to see the lives of disabled people improved, because I know so many people who live lives that are nowhere near what they could be if there was accessible public transport, if there was adequate housing, if they could have access to equal employment, if they could go off and do a degree if they wanted. You see so many people, so much potential, so much to contribute to society wasting away in institutions for example. It needn't be that way; that's what I'm saying.

How such changes might be achieved is a question we need to consider here. One answer might be through the mass mobilisation of disabled people; after all, there are more than 6 million of us, and if we all agreed to vote in the same way, we could determine what any future government might be. Elsewhere one of us has argued that the mass mobilisation of disabled people as a united electoral force is very unlikely indeed (Oliver 1984, 1990), but that does not imply that the collective self-organisation of disabled people does not have enormous potential as a different kind of political force.

IS THE DISABILITY MOVEMENT A MASS MOVEMENT?

We have already discussed the problem of whom exactly the disability movement represents, and we now need to discuss how much support the movement can muster amongst the ranks of disabled people. The reality, as Nasa Begum points out, is that the disability movement, however it is defined, cannot yet claim to be a mass movement, in that some groups of disabled people participate hardly at all at present:

> I hear lots of people say, 'There needs to be a lot done for the young disabled people', and I think that's right, but I think equally there's a lot of older disabled people who are just nowhere, who are just lost.

Alan Pinn is concerned that there is a great need for many more disabled people to become politically active:

> One of the sad things is that there's not enough disabled people willing to get involved in these sort of organisations. And if disabled people don't get off their backsides and do something about it we're going to end up back where we started. So I do think disabled people themselves have got a responsibility to change things. We can't expect things to change without us exerting some pressure ourselves.

People First make a similar point about people with learning difficulties:

> People with learning difficulties should get help and support to speak up for themselves, because there are always some people with learning difficulties who don't realise that one day they will have to learn to speak up for themselves. They're spoken for at present and one day they are not going to be able to sit there. What are they going to do if people ask them to speak? They should be taught how to speak up for themselves and to give each other more support.

Elspeth Morrison is not optimistic about the mass involvement of disabled people:

> The main problem is that we end up mirroring existing political structures and that there's not enough involvement of grass-roots people, although I don't like that term. It makes them sound like vegetables. But because there's so much unravelling and explaining to do, I just don't think there's enough ground swell of support. So we do get bogged down in the few doing the work for the many, for all kinds of reasons, time being one, and also there is an unwillingness to actually hand over power among some disabled people.

There is also the problem of deciding whether to concentrate resources and skills on helping individuals with problems or trying to address the social causes of those problems. This dilemma is faced by many disability activists; should we focus our energies on helping individuals practically or on struggling collectively to achieve broader social changes? Millie Hill feels she is faced with a just such a difficulty: 'I'm still at the stage where I'm so caught up in trying to help individuals out of those situations that I haven't got to the point yet where I can see the wider political context.'

Mike Barrett, speaking from his own immense experience, sees democratic policy formulation mechanisms as crucial to building a mass movement:

> What we have to always ensure is that if you're a mass membership organisation like mine then your members, through their branches, through their area councils and through their conferences, determine policy. When you're sitting at the top you must have regard for that policy all the time, so that when you speak you can produce the evidence in the form of the resolutions, reports etc., and say, 'That is what my members are saying, that's what they passed.'

He goes on to make the point that the BCODP, as an umbrella organisation representing other organisations, is in a different position:

> The BCODP is in a slightly more difficult position. The BCODP has to look at all the organisations it's got and to demonstrate quite clearly that it listens and gives these people the opportu-

nity to produce their policies. Thus when the BCODP is discussing its strategy and the way forward, it has regard for those policies. Where it sees major areas of controversy then they've got to sit down and have some very hard talking between the groups to arrive at a consensus of opinion. You can't just wash it under the table and make an individual statement because nobody can make up their minds. That's the wrong way forward. What will happen then is people will begin to say, 'Well, do we want to belong to this any more?'.

There is also an external dimension to this; even though the disability movement is making great efforts to build accountability, democracy and representation into its self-organisation, the collective voice of disabled people still goes largely unrecognised. Micheline Mason describes the current situation:

> We have not yet had the means to make ourselves known, and we have not yet sufficiently challenged the massive power of the non-disabled charities, the medical officers, the planners, the administrators and the politicians, whose advice is still sought as the 'experts' on disability matters. Individual disabled people can muscle their way into the councils and committees, but almost never as official representatives of disabled people, because we are still not considered to have a collective voice.

IS THE SOCIAL MODEL THE BASIS FOR A MASS MOVEMENT?

Throughout this book, we have emphasised the critical role the social model has had in promoting self-understanding and developing a platform for change. At this point in our history, the adequacy of the social model is being questioned by disabled people themselves (for fuller discussion of this, see Oliver 1995: Ch. 3). The question we address here, particularly in the light of our discussions in the previous chapter, is whether it can provide the theoretical and experiential basis for a mass movement.

Ann MacFarlane suggests that the issue of illness needs to be considered and that, for many disabled people, high-quality medical services are just as important as the removal of social barriers:

I recognise that there are a proportion – it doesn't matter in what proportion that is – of disabled people who are ill and who are disabled. There are many disabled people who want really brilliant medical services because they need them for their lives. They need them in terms of pain control, they need them in terms of pressure sore treatment. I'm just giving those examples to help explain what I'm trying to get across; that there's a debate out there now which is becoming noisier and stronger from those people that we still haven't totally convinced of the social model, who say, 'Well hang on a minute, we've got to have good medical services.'

Vic Finkelstein argues that whatever else we do, we must have some understanding of our own history as well as continuing to develop the social model, otherwise we risk throwing away some of the material and ideological gains we have already made:

A lot of the new generation of disabled people are gaining the benefits but not recognising where it's come from, and as a result they're not participating in the movement. That is a pity really because that weakens it and they really weaken the future, for the future generations. We need to deepen our understanding of the social model, the social approach. Materially I don't think that our gains have been as great as we would wish, and they are connected to just the natural growth of society as such.

TACTICS FOR ACHIEVING CHANGE

If understanding our own history and continually developing the social model are two of the prerequisites for achieving change, then mutual support is a tactical necessity. Nasa Begum makes the point that we have to support each other to achieve meaningful social change:

To get change, to actually fight for our rights, one of the things that we must do is to actually support each other much more. If we support each other much more and enable disabled people to have a better life because we've become positive about who we are, then we can deal with some of the crap that is being thrown at us. Then that's a real achievement.

She goes on to suggest ways in which the BCODP might change its structure in order to facilitate this:

I think organisations like the BCODP should have individual membership and provide forums where disabled people can get together. Maybe not at a high academic level, but actually to talk to each other and give younger disabled people and other disabled people who haven't been involved in the movement a chance.

Nasa recognises that this would be a big change for the BCODP and suggests that it could develop a similar structure to that of the Labour Party:

It would mean quite a big change for the BCODP, but one side of the organisation could be for organisations of disabled people and the other side has individual membership. The Labour Party is partly represented by the unions and the rest is individual membership.

Since these interviews took place, the BCODP has both changed its constitution to allow individual membership and changed its name to the British Council of Disabled People to reflect this. There will still, of course, be differences within the movement which will need to be recognised and provided for organisationally, but ultimately, Nasa Begum suggests, unity is strength:

I actually think there needs to be some room to recognise that disabled women will have specific experiences, as will black disabled people. I am partly a separatist and partly an integrationist in that I do think that disabled people must unite together and fight for our rights collectively. But I do think there needs to be room to enable disabled women to take control and actually articulate some of the debates around our experiences.

Vic Finkelstein, whose thinking has had a profound effect on the development of the movement, is clear about what the key task is, and why it is key:

I would like to see the disability movement developing a national policy on disability. I think that that's an essential thing. What I think is the key and a crucial factor is the way it's developed. If it's developed by a set of experts it will be replicating what DIG does. I think a national disability policy should be a product of mass involvement, and how we do that is the critical thing. That's the thing that I would go for. We should really start by trying to set up committees at all levels to develop and have an input into policy. We can't do that until our movement has spread to a certain stage, but then when it's spread to that stage we could, and that would become part of the growth; people actually participating in developing policy. I could write a policy, you could write a policy, but we've actually got to engage disabled people in that process. My view is the longer we avoid that, the less likely we are to get a proper policy. Instead we're likely to get a policy that's been produced by the elite and then the argument will be to influence government. And then you'll be organising disabled people to put pressure on government, and actually that's precisely what DIG is.

Anne Rae supports this and suggests the BCODP urgently needs to produce a manifesto. She points to the benefits and difficulties this would cause:

I think that the BCODP's biggest failure is not to have published, for want of a better word, a manifesto; a very, very strong policy statement to make clear why people should join the BCODP. Perhaps such a manifesto might have resulted in making the BCODP smaller, but it would have also made it a lot stronger. It might have saved it from spreading itself too thinly in areas where we cannot be effective until we have consolidated very strong policies.

This process has now begun with the organisation of a seminar and the production of a position paper on IL, with other initiatives to follow.

RELATIONSHIPS WITH GOVERNMENT?

The question of policy raises issues about what relationship the movement should have with government and other political institutions. As other social movements have found to their cost, to get too close is to risk incorporation, while to remain too aloof is to risk marginalisation and a slow death because of resource starvation. On this point, Elsa Beckett confesses confusion:

I find it very confusing talking about mainstream politics.

People say, 'You mustn't get one particular political party to take up disability because they'll use it as their football and drop it when they feel like it. You must get cross-party support.' I don't know if that is the right approach or not. I'm very confused about it. Sometimes I think it would have been easier to work on one party and get them to take it up seriously.

Barbara Lisicki believes that tying the movement to one particular party is not the way forward, even in the future:

One possible scenario is that a Labour government will get elected, and then the nature of the battleground will shift because some people will think this is going to be better for us. Now theoretically it should be, but whether it will be or not I don't know. So what we are going to have to do is, and we've said this repeatedly to Labour politicians, 'Once you are in government we are going to be on your doorstep.' This isn't going to stop when a Labour government gets in. We have got to be really, really clear that disabled people have not got a vested interest in any one political party, because we have never been able to trust any of them in the past. It is also previous Labour governments that have instituted some of the oppressive structures that we have got today.

John Evans is clear about the BCODP's relationship to government:

We can't ignore the fact that we have to work with government, whatever that government is, because if we're going to get rights legislation, ADL, in this country we need the support of politicians. We need the support of politicians from all parties, and while that's particularly difficult with the Conservative government in power at the moment, there are politicians, Conservative politicians, that are behind us. We have to work within the political parliamentary structures that we have, even though it's not easy to make changes and it's a long-drawn-out process. But I don't see the BCODP as an organisation ever sitting back and taking what the government says and fitting into it and becoming a RADAR or a 'for' organisation.

And he also points to the need to work with mainland Europe:

In the future I'd like to see the BCODP playing a more positive and prominent role in Europe. It's beginning to, and what's happening is that the BCODP is learning a lesson about how we might become more active and organised. That's partly because some of the other European countries have better provisions than we have, especially in Scandinavia.

Rachel Hurst suggests that the movement in Britain should strengthen its ties with the rest of the world, but is also mindful of the dangers that may bring:

I think the movement in Britain has a particular role to play on the international scene, particularly through its connections with the Commonwealth and with Europe. But there are two things I'm frightened of: one that we get too big, and two that we become an establishment organisation. I don't know how we are going to stop that. I don't think it's going to happen yet because we've still got too much to fight for, but I wish there was some way we could leave messages for the future – 'Don't become an establishment organisation.'

John Evans agrees, and points to the need to work with disabled people from third world countries, despite some of the massive difficulties involved:

It was incredible being able to go and witness and experience Independence 92 in Vancouver – and have contact with lots of disabled people from third world countries, especially Latin America and Africa. Those countries have absolutely nothing. There's not a lot of room to manoeuvre at the moment. When you look at the world economic situation, you realise there are all those Latin American and African countries with massive debts to the western countries. The only way we can overcome it is by the western countries putting more money into those countries to help them develop positively. And if that's not going to happen then disabled people, unfortunately, are going to suffer even more in those countries. So it's quite horrific to think that people generally in those third world countries are suffering anyway, and we all know that disabled people will suffer even more. It's only by working in our own way, by trying to develop the expertise and creativity that we have as disabled people, that we are, in any way, going to overcome the financial, economic problems that we're going to face as disabled people all over the world.

The concern that the disability movement in Britain shows for disability issues throughout the world adds force to our argument that it can be seen as a new social movement; its attempts to organise internationally reflect the increasing globalisation of economic and social life. Our argument is reinforced by the movement's concern with issues which are not impairment- or disability-specific; examples include poverty, exploitation, war and human rights. In order to address these broader issues, the question of building alliances needs to be considered.

BUILDING ALLIANCES?

Ken Davis draws attention to the need to create alliances with other organisations concerned to challenge oppression and bring about social change, but points out that we have to be careful about whom we create alliances with:

> Well there's no real problem for me with that. Disability is a form of social oppression. Social oppression has to be resisted. It has to be overcome. That means social change. Any political orientation which is about preserving the status quo is bound to hold back the process of social change. Therefore I think there's a matter of political alignment with any movement arguing for social change and broadening the political process. That's not to say that organisations on the left of British politics are non-oppressive in relation to disability. Quite the reverse.

Joe Hennessey suggests that as well as building broad alliances, the disability movement ought to co-operate more effectively with traditional disability organisations:

> What I would like to see, without the BCODP in any way diminishing its aims, is the sort of arrangement that exists with VOADL [Voluntary Organisations for Anti-Discrimination Legislation] and the DBC, where people who have a similar view of things are prepared to work together.

Internal alliances among oppressed groups of disabled people should also be on the agenda, according to Nasa Begum:

> We need to get more black people, more lesbians, more women onto the committees and actually get the people who are there to actually start thinking about what they're doing. For

example, their notion of equal opportunities is that we all start on a level playing field. To me it's not about that. It's actually recognising that disabled men are in much more of a powerful position and much more likely to get active. There are different issues for disabled women. So one of the things is that there needs to be a real shake-up on the committees and some work done to actually get people to start thinking about it and maybe getting some stuff written about it as well.

Paddy Ladd suggests a way in which such alliances might be built and cemented:

We would hope that a position paper, explaining deaf culture, history and education, would be written and put to the BCODP, then taken on board and sent to disabled people. We would also like to see this done for each disability group, so that we all have a potted history of their organisations, development, major issues etc. For example, we understand that guide dogs charities are wealthy far in excess of the number of blind people, or dogs required, yet blind people cannot access this money for other urgent needs.

EXPRESSING OUR ANGER THROUGH DIRECT ACTION: DEMONSTRATIONS AND PUBLIC SUPPORT

Various forms of public demonstration have been used by disabled people throughout this century at least. There were mass demonstrations of blind workers and sympathisers in London in 1920, 1933 and 1947, protesting against unemployment, low wages and poor working conditions (Humphreys and Gordon 1992). Subsequently DIG organised a rally in Trafalgar Square in the late 1960s in support of its campaign for a national disability income.

Joe Hennessey reminds us that there was a public demonstration on the issue of personal mobility in 1971: 'On the mobility front, in 1971 I chaired this mass rally in Trafalgar Square seeking a replacement for the invalid tricycle by a small car.' The next major demonstration took place in 1988, and was a march of more than 2,000 disabled people on the offices of the Department of Health and Social Security (DHSS) at the Elephant and Castle. It was organised by the BCODP, which invited other organisations to participate. Not only was it a peaceful public protest but it also became a spontaneous demonstration of civil disobedience, marking another important turning point in our history, as some disabled people decided they were no longer prepared to be nice in airing grievances publicly.

Barbara Lisicki was there and describes the experience:

> I was there at the Elephant and Castle and that was a great, great powerful moment. The Elephant was the DHSS and bloody Nicholas Scott (Minister for Disabled People) was holed up in there or not there at all. Nobody would actually come out and meet the march, even though they had had advance notice of it, received the petition and had a discussion. It just struck me as just so dismissive and disrespectful of disabled people. I just think it bubbled over and blew. People just said, 'How dare you treat us with such contempt.' Everybody just sat down and blocked the Elephant and Castle roundabout. It stopped and blocked the traffic. I thought it was enormously powerful. When you sit down in the road and refuse to move you really are making a statement. We were saying to this guy who is the minister for disabled people, and yet who treats us like we don't exist, if he doesn't think we are important enough then watch out because we will make him know that we are. I think that is the power of direct action, that you can't ignore it. That was a great moment for me and I should say that it was a gas. I loved that demo and I think people got a real buzz out of it.

The late Simon Brisenden, a young disabled activist from Hampshire, was inspired to write the following poem about it:

The battle for the Elephant and Castle

we were sisters and brothers
and a whole bunch of others
not to mention a long line of blue
we were disabled, united
and completely incited
by an anger we knew to be true
we were 2000 strong
and half a mile long
as we marched to the Elephant and Castle
with no sight or no hearing
a kaleidoscope careering
filling the sky with our voices
we marched down the street

to tell the elite
we demand a world with new choices
we had in our sights
a blow for our rights
as we marched to the Elephant and Castle
we were at the beginning
of a new way of winning
together we could not be denied
so we strolled up and down
in old London town
wearing our badges with pride
we fought the law
and we'll fight it some more
at every other Elephant and Castle

It is not just that such demonstrations get the attention of wider society; they are also a very empowering experience. Patricia Rock describes her initial forays into direct action, when she and others disrupted women's meetings because they failed to take the needs of disabled women into account:

It was the first time I'd done that and I had a megaphone, there were no mikes or anything, and I had to shout from the back of the hall and say we were unrepresentative. Mich [Mason] was there and they said I could speak at the end and not speak now. Anyway I stopped the meeting. It was very powerful. So we stopped the meeting, and after that Sue [Fairclough] and I went to meetings virtually every Saturday and stopped them. We got people to carry us up steps and we'd stop the meeting. There were usually no microphones so you just had to shout. It was often me shouting because Sue just didn't have a strong enough voice, although she had the political arguments. So I became sort of like the spokesperson. We decided that we had quite a lot of things to say so we started SAD, Sisters Against Disablement.

Alan Holdsworth talks about how recent campaigns for accessible transport have had an empowering effect on the previously disempowered:

The actions that DAN does, like the Cardiff one [in the city centre in March 1995], are just so powerful. There were disabled people there who have no idea of the social model but they're empowered, right, and maybe now they're learning a bit about the social model as well. Even if they are not, they are certainly coming to the next demonstration.

Patricia Rock expresses the hope that direct action will become a more focused and central tactic within the movement: 'My hopes are that the movement is becoming more radical in terms of direct action. I'm a great believer in direct action and I hope that the BCODP will be in the forefront of it.' Alan Holdsworth agrees, and does not think direct action is something only one organisation should actually do:

> I've got no problems with the BCODP authorising direct action if necessary, or the Integration Alliance, or whoever. And if they want DAN's help or advice or support or connections, we're quite happy to share them. I don't see everything has to come through DAN. I think the media see that, but it's up to other groups to push themselves into the media.

Getting attention is, suggests Patricia Rock, the main point of direct action; initially the attention of the media, and then that of the general public:

> The more oppression you get, the more angry you are and the more need there is to speak out, so that hopefully we'll get more press coverage, and we're beginning to get people to realise and change their attitudes around disabled people in this country. That's my hope; that the 1990s will really see us getting to where the Americans were in the 1970s; you know, taking over tower blocks and sit-ins, really coming into the public eye's focus.

Alan Holdsworth, however, emphasises the crucial difference between actions and campaigns:

> You have to have a campaign, it's not like an action. It's not about going out making your point and coming home and that's it. Clearly with the accessible public transport issue, we've got to stick to the campaign; that is, a series of actions, a series of battles in the war. So, at the moment we have raised the issue of transport on the agenda, and the government is about to start asking, 'What do you want?'. Then we issue the demands and these are reasonable, giving the government quite a long time for them to be met. I think that's the sort of thing that the public want to see, so it puts more pressure on

the government because there is a plan and it's pretty logical what we're setting down. And you focus on transport until you win.

Joe Hennessey also sees the mass media as important and suggests that, at present, disabled people are quite well served and have an active involvement in programme making: 'The fact is that we've now got some good media outlets and with programmes that disabled people themselves are involved in making. These state our case and can challenge all the other things that are going on.' When they do, he is optimistic that support from the general public will be forthcoming:

> I'm quite sure that there is a great deal of support from Mr Him and Her out there when they realise what the issues are. I'm talking about the population at large, who don't tend to think about disability issues, but when they're confronted by them they can see the discrimination and can see the unfairness. Then it does tweak people's consciences. We've just got to keep on doing that. We've got to go on fighting regardless.

It is important to note that while the record of the mass media is not good as far as disability representation is concerned, specialist programmes, such as *LINK* in particular, have made a very valuable contribution to developing and sustaining the movement. Paddy Ladd acknowledges this:

> We also got some co-operation from the *LINK* programme, whose historical importance should not be underrated, and they enabled up to put across some of our views on the place of deaf schools and BSL over two full-length programmes.

The *LINK* programme was indeed the vanguard of disability programming in the UK. With Rosalie Wilkins presenting and co-producing with Richard Creasey (a well-established television executive producer), an important disabled/non-disabled alliance was made. A magazine programme that responded to the lead of the emerging disability movement was key. Their first ever programme featured Vic Finkelstein talking about the social model. This was remarkably ahead of its time, and consistent with *LINK*'s underlying policy, from which it has never deviated in twenty-two years. The policy was to give a platform to disabled people, their organisations and campaigns and to provide information.

Rosalie Wilkins reflects on the emergence of the *LINK* programme:

> I met Richard Creasey, who was starting this disability programme. Originally he was doing it in very traditional terms. I introduced him to Vic, who taped the whole meeting and gave him such a hard time. Richard was so good, and you could hear his desperation in trying to catch up with these thoughts and being excited by them at the same time. Anyway, that very much turned *LINK* around, and Vic was on the very first programme talking about the social model.

As *LINK* was located within a documentary department, they were also able to make programmes like *We Won't Go Away*, a fifty-minute piece depicting the American disability movement's struggle for ADL, and *Statement of Intent*, which followed the year-long campaign by DCDP to secure themselves a base for their CIL. Both programmes had a profoundly inspiring effect on disabled people trying to establish their own local and national powerbase and campaigning strategies.

Rosalie Wilkins modestly evaluates the importance of *LINK* to the movement:

> I'd like to think that it was important in giving people experience of dealing with the media, of exposure to it. The documentaries that went along with it – *We Won't Go Away*, for example – wouldn't have been made if *LINK* hadn't been there, and the same goes for *Statement of Intent*. Richard and later Pat [Ingram] always recognised the importance of the growing movement and feel very proud of that.

Today *LINK* has been joined but not superseded by the creation of other dedicated series or documentaries informed and produced by disabled people, committed to reporting on disability as a social issue. A specific Disability Unit was established within the BBC and a similar limited project at Channel 4, to train disabled people to become skilled in research, directing and producing, to encourage a transition or integration of our ideas and expertise into the general media machine. Hence, in recent years, we have seen more documentaries focused on our civil rights and denial of those rights rather than the 'triumph over tragedy' genre that has dogged our media representation since its beginning.

However, David Hevey, who works in television, sounds a warning against complacency as far as the media is concerned:

> While you will get a growth in disability culture, and things like the Disability Programmes Unit at the BBC, they may actually eclipse real struggle because such developments will appear to have been the results of real struggle. For example, an exhibition may cost £1,000 or £2,000, whereas ramping a building may cost around £20,000. On a basic level you may get a cultural response where you don't actually get physical access, in order to fob off people.

DEMOCRACY IS COMING...

Despite all the difficulties that the disability movement has faced, Maggie and Ken Davis are confident both of its survival and of its increasing influence and importance:

> In the 1990s the movement is going to come into its own because the ability of government and the other organisations who have traditionally controlled the direction of disability policy in the past is going to come under so much pressure merely as a result of the BCODP's growth and activity. It will mean that there will be an increasing role for the BCODP. You might say that every moment for the BCODP, every step along the way, is a critical moment because everything seems to hang on such a fragile ability to service its own needs. So far it's come through some of the worst battles that any organisation could possibly go through. There have been times in the BCODP when it has had no resources, only the resources of its members, and its members have sustained it through those difficult times in the past.

The key reason for this, as they point out, is that disabled people are citizens too, and therefore, in a representative democracy, it is perfectly appropriate that we have representative organisations to represent us:

> We are part of British society and we're struggling to be equal participative members of it. It's a proper thing that we should

have an organisation at a national level to reflect our local, regional and national interests.

REFORM OR REVOLUTION?

There is then a key question about how change is to come about. Ann MacFarlane is convinced that it has to be through the mass involvement of disabled people: 'You can't expect half a dozen people to change a nation. That's what you're talking about, and nobody can do that.' She also takes the position that existing non-representative organisations will not disappear and therefore they have to be worked with. In her case, she discusses her own single-impairment organisation, Arthritis Care:

> I'm not going to abolish it and nor is anyone else. However much I would like to think I can abolish it, I'm not going to be able to do that. I've watched it go through a period where I wouldn't touch it with a barge pole, but now I see a difference. The fact is that I sat for at least two days working on how we were going to change the complexion of the organisation, how we were going to get that percentage of disabled people along to it. Now we're still talking about segregation, we're still talking about people with all one type of impairment, but if we can change the complexion then I think we have a massive chance, because there's a lot of understanding of the politics of disability within that organisation.

Richard Wood also agrees with the need for co-operation, but within very strict boundaries. Discussing the BCODP's relationship with RADAR, the other umbrella disability organisation, he asserts:

> I don't think there's any question of RADAR and the BCODP coming together. We may join each other in a conference or we may join each other on a benefits consortium or whatever. There is no point in which we can come together; absolutely none at all, any more than DPI and RI can come together. And it's the same issue. If RI and RADAR want to give us unconditionally all their resources for us to do what we like with, that's fine. Short of that, I wouldn't consider it worth discussing. As far as I'm concerned, what we say to them is, 'You do your thing and we'll do our thing. Let's just talk about issues.' But a marriage!

As to hopes about what broad social changes might occur, Ann MacFarlane lays down her own extensive list:

My hope is first of all that we'll get ADL, in which we'll start the process of a greater depth of change or a greater awareness, hopefully, of what needs to be done and how far we've got to go. But I suppose I keep looking at the thing in the historical perspective, and in a way that's why I get stuck, because if you see how slowly the changes are in some places. We think lots has happened, but some of the things are so slow, and you can only move certain things on at a certain pace. Some things you can move on much more quickly, other things you can't. There are disabled people unpoliticised and there's masses and masses of work to do. That's not going to come overnight. My feeling is that if we can get the segregated school system changed, if we can get more work done around structures and consultation and representation within committees and so on at local and national level, then the walls will start to crumble. But I still think that is a two-generation process. While I actually don't agree with specific organisations for specific impairments, if we can change them to the 'ofs', there will then be the movement towards the crumble because there will be a knock-on effect.

Alan Holdsworth is both optimistic about what might be achieved in the foreseeable future and realistic about what will remain to be done:

I think in ten years we'll have civil rights, for sure. We'll have a platform of civil rights and they won't be allowed to deny us access. I think in fifteen years we will have closed every residential centre down, and we'll have a very powerful movement. I think we'll be very politically sensitive, and I think increasingly as the population ages we'll still have an enormous fight on in our old age to just get services.

One of Jenny Morris's hopes focuses on the BCODP itself:

I hope that the BCODP gets more serious about how people perceive it as an organisation. I'm not being very positive because I don't actually feel that positive about it as an organisation currently. Again, I do understand why it is like it is. In many ways the BCODP seems to behave like an organisation under siege sometimes. That's what it feels like and that's part of the reality, so I'm not blaming it, it's under-standable. Maybe the more progress the BCODP makes in terms of its demands and in terms of it being recognised as a legitimate organisation, and as disability is recognised as a legitimate civil rights issue, then maybe it will behave less as an organisation under siege and will be able to draw people in more.

Phillip Mason hopes that the BCODP will continue to stick to its principles as it has done up to now:

The important thing is that it's stuck to its principles. That's really, really very, very important, even though it wasn't a raving popular movement in 1981. It didn't have a great, mass support from disabled people then. Nevertheless it stuck to its guns. It stuck to its primary purpose, and the validity and the integrity of the organisation have meant it flourished. It has done this because it stuck to the principle that disabled people must speak for disabled people. We must have a collective responsibility. Because it's stuck to that it's flourished. And I think that's a great success. It hasn't compromised. It could have compromised quite easily. Look what's happened to the Dutch disability movement. They took over their equivalent of RADAR and in doing so they are compromised and look at them now. Where are they? They have no integrity. They are very wealthy, very rich, very powerful but they're a bunch of professionals. They don't speak for disabled people. That's the great thing about the BCODP, it's never compromised. It's stuck to its guns and you've got to admire it for that. And it's the stronger for it now.

Colin Low, while admitting the achievements of the BCODP, is concerned about its future:

I do not minimise the achievements of the BCODP. Its way of working has done much to draw attention to disability issues and get them on the agenda, and has done much to raise the status of disabled people in discussion of disability issues. But a failure to address issues of the priority to be accorded to questions of status versus service provision, and co-operation versus opposition, has meant that the goal of acting as a focus for the whole disability movement has to date remained unrealised. In fact for the reasons I have given it has begun to unravel at international level, and the same thing is likely to occur at national level before very much longer.

He has a much more pluralist vision of future developments:

As for the future, I think we are likely to see a more pluralistic disability movement composed of a number of elements which are formally independent of one another and pursue their independent policies and objectives, but which co-operate with one another round the central core of issues, like ADL, which are of concern to all disability organisations.

The disability movement does not of course exist in a vacuum, and the harder it pushes for change, the more successful it becomes, the more resistance it is likely to encounter. Ann MacFarlane makes this point:

I feel there's a lot of things that are subtly, almost insidiously, slipping away. A couple of years back I felt that hands were coming out to somewhere meet us along the way and I almost began to have a hope that we were going to be valued. But I'm beginning to feel very much that the hands that were coming towards us from the non-disabled groupings are still concerned about themselves in all of the political debates and that we're going to be pushed away again. I just don't feel very confident about that.

THE BATTLE FOR IDEAS MAY BE WON

Phillip Mason suggests that the battle for ideas may already be won:

I feel like a 21-year-old, the world is our oyster, and I really believe that for disabled people. One of the major achievements of the BCODP is that the intellectual argument is won. Society accepts the rightness, the truth of the BCODP's arguments. Civil rights issues at a heart-felt level are accepted, although perhaps not at a practical level, as we see with Telethon. But you talk to ordinary people, you talk to young people nowadays, and they accept entirely what the BCODP is saying. We have a society that is open to disabled people taking control of their own lives. Unfortunately many of the structures that will enable that are still overtly or covertly opposed; not least the fact that our country is poorer and it sees its priorities as elsewhere. We might have won the intellectual battle but nevertheless, in a practical everyday level, the old practices persist.

He does go on to suggest, however, that there are opposing ideological forces which are involved in shaping society's ideas about disabled people:

We've got to remember that most disabled people are still in family or marriage situations where they're looked after by spouse or relatives. The 'carers' lot' have stolen the march on us to some extent and there's a certain friction developing between the carers' lobby and disabled people. We tend to be portrayed by them as being mean, manipulative, demanding, ungrateful, and burdens.

Sian Vasey is concerned that the nature of disability is still misunderstood throughout society:

It seems to me that everywhere there is this huge misunderstanding about disability. There's almost no understanding about disability and it doesn't matter where you go. Go to the Communist Party, go to the Labour Party, go to the Conservative Party; wherever you go, there's almost uniform ignorance.

And Phillip Mason himself is not so hopeful about the way ideas are being developed in practice. He also points out what many disabled people have found to our cost over the years: that others are very good at stealing our ideas; and he further suggests that, on occasions, these very ideas may be used to oppress us:

Because many of the old practices persist and simply because you've got conflicts of interest, those conflicts are coming out. What's tending to happen is our clothes are being taken off us and being used in the process of oppression. One of the things we learnt a lot in Le Court is that actually the system has a great capacity for taking your ideas and reinterpreting them to their own benefit. The whole idea of resident participation was something that Paul Hunt fought for, and he'd be appalled to see how it's been used and manipulated actually so as to enable the oppressor further to control the lives of disabled people.

WHAT KIND OF A SOCIETY DO WE WANT?

It might be more appropriate to put the question at the head of this section the other way round, because, while many disabled people may not have a fully worked out vision of the kind of society they want to live in, they know the kind of society they do not want in the future. Richard Wood is clear about the kind of society he does not want:

> There are a lot of things that are very worrying in society today. Some of these may be cyclical, to do with economic recessions, but there are other issues I find even more disturbing. The increasing openness of the debate around the quality of life I find extremely disturbing, and the fact that many academics are now quite happy to sit in open forums and talk about who has the right to live and the right to die. We shouldn't pretend it's any other discussion, it's not about resources. Genetic engineering, euthanasia; these are all very disturbing things that may be cyclical, but we can't work on the assumption that they are.

Phillip Mason suggests that even relatively narrow battles raise enormous questions for the kind of society we might want:

> Why should 'society' have concern for its underprivileged? It's a debate that's got to come. The basis on which we are arguing for direct payments is that it enables disabled people to have an equal opportunity to participate in society. Thereafter you've got to leave disabled people to exercise the responsibilities and opportunities that any other citizen does. And that's what I feel about getting down to basic issues. We argue for direct funding as being a way to enable equal opportunity. Now whether or not society is prepared to enable equal opportunity is a debate that's got to take place. At the moment we have politicians saying that they care for us and then they decide how and where, when and to what extent. But we've got to say, 'That's wrong. If you care for us then we should define and decide.'

He goes on to argue that freedom of speech and thought are essential, and that 'right on' disabled people should not oppress other disabled people:

> We have got to be clear what we stand for, what we believe in, and we've got to be confident that what we stand for and believe in is the truth and it will come through. That's why the strength of the BCODP over the last ten years is that it has been

speaking the truth, and the truth's come through, and gradually it's dawning on society at large. But even now we mustn't become the new oppressors. We mustn't establish institutions that prescribe. We must fight for the right of individual disabled people to disagree with us violently. We might disagree with what they stand for, but we've got to fight for their rights as human beings, and that's very hard because it would appear as if we're working against our own interest. But they're human beings and they're as entitled as we are to have their point of view, even though we think ours is the truth. One of the struggles for the future for the BCODP is that it must not become the new oppressor. It must not.

Micheline Mason wants us to be putting the building blocks of a new society into place to be ready for the collapse of capitalism, whenever it may come:

> The right to take part in society as equals is meaningless whilst the levels of inequality between non-disabled people are so vast and growing. Capitalism is now world-wide and collapsing, its wealth becoming concentrated in fewer and fewer hands, whose owners are becoming more desperate with every 'crisis'. I am still longing for a forum in which disabled people take leadership over world-wide issues, where we can think, feel and learn together. I am bored with the victim role. I want to model a better way of relating to each other than that offered by the non-disabled world, and I want to have new kinds of organisational forms in place before the collapse of capitalism makes everyday survival too difficult and time-consuming to organise ourselves.

CONCLUSIONS: IS THE BCODP PUTTING THE BUILDING BLOCKS OF A NEW SOCIETY INTO PLACE?

According to Richard Wood, the BCODP is now beginning to move from responding to agendas set by others to setting our own agendas:

> I think from 1990 onwards we've now started to move into a position of saying, 'Well now we've arrived, let's find out where we're going.' I think things like our taking control over research, for example, might be a way of saying, 'Look, now we are taking control of these issues.' We're saying we have the

solutions to our agenda, not those that other people set for us, which has been the position in the past. I remember in the [Derbyshire] CIL we often went in like that. What the BCODP and increasingly some of the more established member organisations are doing is setting the agenda. What we're doing, through things like our research into discrimination and the four or five major research programmes that we've got at the moment going, is moving into a position of setting the agenda and from that agenda being able to say, 'OK, well, where are we going with it, then?', and taking over the issue. That's a radical move from the way that we might have addressed the issues four or five years ago.

One item on the agenda set by the BCODP has been civil rights legislation. This now, according to Wood (and we agree), is inevitable, but it poses the question, 'After it – what?':

There is the broader question of civil rights legislation. I believe that legislation is imminent. I wouldn't wish to put a date on what I mean as imminent, but I think that it will happen; it's a question of when, and not if, any more. The whole question around what shape that legislation will take has got to be a key issue for the BCODP into the future. But more fundamentally, when the legislation is passed we have got to continue to build a movement.

The education of both disabled people and the general public is also part of the new agenda being set by the BCODP, according to Wood:

I think the second role that the BCODP has to play on a national front is that of education. The BCODP has to, in the very near future, discover a way of telling people the truth (I'm talking about society now, not just disabled people) about the issues that we face. And also telling people the truth about the real contribution that disabled people are making, and can make, to society. To change this stereotype of disabled people as recipients and being people who everyone else is paying their taxes for, to saying, 'Well, that's not true, is it; disabled people can contribute, and would contribute, so much to society if they were enabled to.' So part of that educative process has got to be strengthened, and I think they are really two of our major roles: empowering disabled people and educating people.

Chapter 9

The disability movement
Is it a new social movement?

> The great majority of human beings who have been at history's margins will come into their own and create a new history, which while still imperfect will contain more positive elements and exhibit fewer errors.
>
> (Gramsci quoted in Lyman 1995b: 411)

INTRODUCTION

The 1980s began with IYDP and was designated as the Decade of Disabled People by the United Nations (UN). Despite the fact that the decade has been virtually ignored by governments, statutory and voluntary bodies alike, disabled people have made it the most important and significant decade in their history. All over the world, they have built their own organisations. The first half of the 1990s has seen this as a base on which a collective disability movement has been built. To put this in the terminology of this book, the emerging disability movement has now emerged.

However, the fact that the movement has now emerged does not mean that disabled people can sit back and enjoy the fruits of their collective labours. In Britain we must build on the legacy of UPIAS, as it no longer exists. Richard Wood, as Director of the organisation that in some ways could be said to have inherited the mantle of UPIAS, pays tribute:

> UPIAS, in its own way, was a focus. It was a small group and I suppose, in hindsight, it was a fairly elite group. But that seems to be the case with the birth of most civil rights movements. Here you had a group of people that not only started to recognise that there were problems and issues to be addressed

but who were actually starting to redefine them into what we now accept as the social model of disability.

As we have already suggested, one of the important aspects of building on what has gone before is that we have some proper accounts of the issues that were raised and the ways in which they were dealt with; hence one purpose of this book. However, our purpose has been not just to make a contribution to the history of disabled people's self-organisation, but also to provide an analysis of the significance of this in the context of the rise of new social movements in the late twentieth century. We will do this both by continuing to use the words of disabled people themselves and by placing them in a framework developed by analysts of these movements.

AN EVALUATION OF THE DISABILITY MOVEMENT ITSELF

According to Marx and McAdam (1994), there are four criteria against which any social movement (new or not) must be judged. These are whether any new political or economic changes have resulted from its activities, whether any specific legislation has resulted, what changes in public opinion and behaviour have been produced, and whether any new organisations or institutions have been created. However, as we have argued throughout this book that the disability movement is a new social movement, so there are three further criteria against which the movement should be evaluated. These are the extent of consciousness raising and empowerment amongst disabled people, the extent to which disability issues are raised internationally, and the promotion of disability as a human and civil rights issue.

New political or economic changes

It is difficult to provide hard evidence that, at present, the activities of disabled people in Britain have produced substantial improvements in their lives. The work of Barnes (1991), using data from a wide range of official sources, demonstrates that the majority of disabled people in Britain lead lives that are significantly worse than those of their non-disabled counterparts. Joe Hennessey relates this situation to his own experience: 'You could say that I was an angry young man. I still am angry. I'm an angry middle-aged man now; because there is still so much that is grotesquely wrong; because of the constant lies of the politicians.'

In international terms, the situation is even bleaker. A recent UN report (Despouy 1993) confirmed earlier estimates that there are more than 500 million impaired persons in the world; that is one in ten of the world's population. The report goes on to suggest that:

> These persons frequently live in deplorable conditions, owing to the presence of physical and social barriers which prevent their integration and full participation in the community. As a result, millions of disabled people throughout the world are segregated and deprived of virtually all their rights, and lead a wretched, marginal life.
>
> (Despouy 1993: 1)

Clearly then much needs to be done to improve the material conditions under which disabled people live throughout the world. It would be wrong to conclude from this, however, that the disability movement has failed to achieve any economic or political changes. To begin with, the movement is very young and is still struggling against the old, traditional approaches based upon the individualisation and medicalisation of disability. Additionally, the movement has succeeded in giving a voice to disabled people and making sure that this voice is heard at the relevant political and economic fora throughout the world. The crucial issue for the movement over the next few years is to make sure this collective voice is not merely heard but taken notice of.

Specific legislation

In terms of the legislative impact of the movement, there are two issues that need to be considered. First, there is the impact that the movement has had upon the existing legislative programmes of government. Over the years, the movement has been able to make a contribution in this area without becoming solely a parliamentary lobby group or becoming too closely identified with the political process. Rachel Hurst sums up the movement's contribution thus:

> The input that we did have was important to the legislation at

that time. The fact that we were, by that time, part of all that was important. Equally the fact that more and more disabled people were able to hear what it is that it's all about was important.

However, as Anne Rae points out, even where disabled people are able to make an input into the legislative process, there is no guarantee that the legislation will be of much use:

All this fine-sounding stuff about the ideology of community care, unless the government gets its act together and starts supporting people properly in the community, the backlash is going to be so bad that retrieving anything from it is going to take the work of very committed people. It is going to take a lot of energy and resources that could leave us quite weak because people, rightly or wrongly, have put a lot of faith into the Community Care Act and look at it as some kind of step to liberation.

The major impact that the movement in Britain has had has been in terms of the promotion of the idea of what was initially ADL but has now become civil rights legislation. While this is not yet on the statute books, the movement has succeeded in converting all of the political parties and the vast majority of voluntary organisations to the idea of legislation to outlaw discrimination. This is no small achievement when put in context: only fifteen years ago, some of these organisations were antagonistic to the issue, and the vast majority were implacably opposed.

There is a final area where the movement has succeeded in producing new legislation, and that is in the promotion of IL by making it legal to pay disabled people cash to purchase their own personal assistance (PA) services. Richard Wood describes the way the movement brought this about:

One of the best things that the BCODP did was to set up the Independent Living Group [ILG] and have people who do use PA services, and hence understand what all that means, not only direct the research, but provide the solutions and point to the way forward. I see the BCODP as a facilitator of that, as a vehicle that will allow people to come together, create the environment where they will come together, and project the arguments that they asked us to project.

Direct payments to disabled people, which have been illegal since the National Assistance Act of 1948, will be legalised in 1996, and that is solely attributable to the disability movement.

Changes in public opinion and behaviour

Judging the extent of changes in public attitudes and behaviour is a very difficult task, particularly in an area like disability where there is very little research evidence on which to make a judgement. John Evans points out that disability is often a neglected issue:

> It would be nice to see disability raised up the agenda a little bit more. But it's not going to be that easy because, while in the case of environmentalism everybody can identify with it, it is not the case that everybody identifies with disability. Even though there is the idea that it can happen to anybody and to a certain extent it does affect everybody, people don't necessarily relate to it in that way. It's trying to develop those things a bit more so that they become higher up the public agenda.

This interview took place before the civil rights campaigns that took place in 1994 and 1995 and the proliferation of peaceful civil rights demonstrations orchestrated by DAN. These have clearly had a major impact on public opinion at least, and, aside from a minor right-wing backlash, there is overwhelming support for disabled people to be given the full entitlements of citizenship. From editorial support in the tabloid newspapers to the support of the inconvenienced public at demonstrations, it is clear that public opinion now recognises the discrimination disabled people face and supports the campaign of the disability movement to eradicate it.

The creation of new organisations and institutions

One of the central issues in any evaluation of the disability movement is whether organisations such as the BCODP constitute new organisational forms. Stephen Bradshaw, while endorsing the principle that disabled people must do it for themselves, does not see the creation of new organisations as the only way ahead:

> I'm a great believer in peaceful revolution and the idea that there's no way to salvation except through toil. But the idea that

you can only get to god my way; that you can only get to Nirvana through the BCODP – that's impossible. Not that I'm a religious person.

He goes on to suggest that the conversion of the old, traditional organisations for disabled people into democratic and accountable ones is also a realistic possibility. 'It's been done with GLAD [Greater London Association of Disabled People] and for different reasons RNIB is actually fairly close. RADAR is getting closer all the time.'

Richard Wood does not agree and reaffirms the principles of accountability and democracy:

The BCODP is a grassroots organisation. We must always hold onto that. The BCODP is not the tail that wags the dog. The dog is its member organisations; that is what we are at the end of the day. We're an important tail, but we only exist because our member organisations exist and will us to exist to carry out a role that they've defined for us. The thing to realise is that in terms of our ability as disabled people to tackle the issues, present the solutions, we have to refer back to the grass roots. We have to refer back to the people who are living with discrimination day to day.

He goes on to suggest that, unlike the traditional organisations, the BCODP has always managed to remain independent of what he calls 'the establishment': 'One of the things that we can be proud of in the BCODP is that actually we've never gone down that road of being part of the establishment.'

David Hevey suggests that the disability movement is a different kind of political movement from others, especially working-class movements, because of their tendencies to be run by elites in their own interests:

I don't accept the genuineness of the struggle of the labour movement; I don't accept that the parliamentary vanguard, if you want to call it that, actually seriously wants to represent the working class. I don't believe that, I think they represent the management class. I believe the vanguard of the disability movement, however posh they are, actually essentially represents the fundamental principle of access for all disabled people.

Throughout this study we have argued that the disability movement is not just a social movement, it is a new social movement. Therefore it is necessary to refer to three other criteria already mentioned in our evaluation of the movement. The first of those concerns the need to educate the followers of the movement to appropriate levels of consciousness in order to unite around a common set of ideas or values.

Empowerment, consciousness raising and education

In evaluating how far the disability movement has come in education and consciousness raising, we must remember the situations in which many, possibly even still a majority of, disabled people are placed. Patricia Rock graphically reminds us:

> The majority of them are not given the opportunity to become politicised, they're stuffed away in day centres and institutions and they're individualised, and their services are individualised. My great hope is that we will allow disabled people to feel that there is someone that speaks for them; that they feel they can be party to. Our historical fate has been divide and rule – services for the mentally ill, services for the mentally handicapped, and services for this and that. We've got to realise that we've got to throw the cake away; in fact there isn't a cake. We want to create something that's new. We've got to think collectively. Most disabled people don't think collectively.

Rachel Hurst makes a similar point, arguing that we are socialised in particular ways and we need to throw off the shackles of this socialisation collectively: 'So many of us fulfil our stereotyped destinies and we need to show that we shouldn't. We don't need to. If there wasn't this constant feeling of negativity about disability or negativity about impairment.' She focuses on the rejection of 'the cure' as part of the collective consciousness-raising exercise: 'All of us are saying we don't want to be cured because actually we think we're better people as disabled people than we were when we weren't.'

Elspeth Morrison points out that the movement has set up its own structures, to educate not only members of the movement itself but others as well:

> Some disabled people work in the industry of disability, doing

disability equality training. There's a career path, which there wasn't say ten years ago. My hopes for the future would be that we pull more people on board and that more disabled people are made aware of their situation, made aware that they are not alone in how they experience the world.

Thus, despite the many difficulties involved, it is clear that an arts and cultural movement has established itself within the disability movement more generally. While the precise nature of its achievements may be difficult to estimate, it has raised the issue of 'disability pride' and made many disabled people feel that they do not have to be ashamed of or apologise for their impairments. This educative process has undoubtedly been an empowering one.

Internationalism

Another factor which distinguishes new movements from others is that they often have international dimensions and they raise important issues for the global community to deal with, not simply for nation states. According to Richard Wood, a collective inter-national movement has collective international responsibilities:

> The recognition, which is now becoming a global recognition, is that economic situations vary, degrees of oppression vary profoundly, but basically we do all face the same forms of discrimination. I think that we have a responsibility in countries where we have democracy to present the issues for people in countries where they don't, and are unable to do so for a variety of reasons.

One way of achieving this is to move beyond the social model of disability, formulated in the context of particular kinds of society, and to develop approaches relevant to disabled people all over the world:

> Now the movement is moving forward into saying, 'This is not just a social model of disability, it's a human rights model of disability.' The next few years are going to be about defining what that model is and what implications it has for our own national movements and the international movement. The BCODP has a major role to play in Europe, and the DPI has a major role to play in the world: in tackling the UN Commission

on Human Rights and through the EEC [European Economic Community].

Human rights, civil rights and citizenship

This leads to the final criterion against which new social movements should be evaluated: the extent to which they can secure human and civil rights for their membership. Richard Wood points out the need to build up alliances with other organisations campaigning around rights issues:

I'm very excited about links that the BCODP is now making with people like Liberty. I'm also very excited that at last we may have the chance to educate them, because I think that in terms of disability issues they need some serious education. But at least that forum is starting to open up and the BCODP will be paying a key role in that. It augurs well for the future. It also augurs well for our ability to maintain our position as a radical but constructive voice of disabled people, a voice that can now work alongside other civil rights groups. It will enable us to retain the vision. The old saying is, 'If you haven't got a mission, you're not going anywhere.' I think having that vision of equality for all citizens is our mission.

He goes on to link this to the internationalism of the movement and the spin-offs that this produces at the national level:

The setting up of the DPI Human Rights Task Force is a very, very significant step, because it moves disability issues into a new dimension. We're even starting to see that in this country. It is now commonplace to hear people talking about human rights when talking about disability. The two things just naturally go together now, and even talking to the government we're talking about human rights – we're not talking about disability issues. I think that is really profound.

Wood, however, is suspicious of going down the road of rights only: 'The danger is that we lose our identity to just a mish-mash of broad human rights issues.' It is perhaps worth noting that many years ago Marx was suspicious of the concept of rights, particularly in its bourgeois and liberal formulations, suggesting that the eradication of class conflict would lead to the fulfilment of human nature and make protective-rights-based legislation unnecessary (Freeden 1991).

WHICH WAY NOW?

While not everyone is as suspicious as they might be about the civil rights framework, Jones (1994), building upon the Marxist critique, goes even further than suspicion:

> Civil rights are a liberal conception of 'equality' which allows the State (despite social policy) to legitimately police its subjects all the same, regardless of our diverse human needs. As such they are a device for making uniform all the rightful demands of the populace on socially-produced value.
>
> (Jones 1994: 31)

We share some of those concerns, but as we hope we have demonstrated in this book, we depart from his characterisation of the strategies of the movement as having nothing more than an uncritical faith in parliamentary democracy generally and civil rights legislation in particular. His claim that the movement has 'an unreflective, fetishised faith in parliaments, civil rights and citizenship' (Jones 1994: 35) is simply not borne out by the facts and the achievements of the movement in terms of consciousness raising, collective empowerment, the building of a disability culture, and the placing of IL on the welfare agenda, to name only some of its extra-parliamentary achievements.

Jones is also wildly inaccurate in his claim that the disability movement as a new social movement can achieve what it wants by developing a cosy relationship with government; or, as he puts it, 'majestically colonise the pluralist state' (Jones 1994: 36). Throughout this book, many leaders of the movement have demonstrated their cautiousness in respect of its relationship with the state and their awareness of the dangers of becoming part of the disability establishment.

Further, his own claim that 'the emancipation of disabled people can only be gained through joint struggles with organisations of the working class' (Jones 1994: 36) flies in the face of history. Indeed, the trade union movement's reactionary response to the Disabled Person's (Employment) Act 1944, which it maintained for nearly fifty years, was based not upon a Marxist critique of legal rights but on a deliberate strategy to further the interests of its non-disabled members.

Finally, the vast majority of disabled people find it hard to distinguish between the benevolent paternalism of the Labour Party (in both its old and new versions) and the paternalistic benevolence of the Tories. It is clear that the party system no longer provides the opportunity for a working-class political force to develop and, as many contributors to this book have emphasised, even if this were not the case, the disability movement would not tie itself to one party only, no matter what it promised.

Another critic is Shakespeare, who, while acknowledging the achievements of the disability movement, doubts whether analyses which conceptualise it as a new social movement are very useful:

> In making 'personal troubles' into 'public issues', disabled people are affirming the validity and importance of their own identity, rejecting both the victimising tendencies of society at large and their own socialisation.... New social movement theory, in combining divergent political phenomena, and overstressing the novelty of these developments, fails usefully to theorise this process.
>
> (Shakespeare 1993: 264)

Instead he suggests that the disability movement should be conceptualised as a liberation movement, because its 'struggles are crucially concerned with economic exploitation and poverty' (Shakespeare 1993: 258). Clearly, such struggles have been a crucial part of the disability movement, but, as we have shown, it has been about much more besides. And if one characterises the disability movement in the way he does, it is hard to see how it differs from DIG and the DA, which are only concerned with economic exploitation and poverty.

Not everyone is as critical of the way the movement has been conceptualised, and many have focused on its achievements. Sally French, for example, sees mutual support as the most important outcome of the movement:

> Perhaps the most important achievement of the disability movement is the powerful impact it has had on disabled people themselves. Disabled people have been internally oppressed by

their conditioning. This has given rise to negative feelings about themselves and other disabled people, similar to those held by the non-disabled world. One of the major achievements of the disability movement is the support it offers disabled people in ridding themselves of this oppression.

(French 1994: 80)

Frances Hasler suggests that the movement has done nothing less than change the meaning of disability for everyone:

During the 1980s the disabled people's movement has changed the discourse on disability in Britain. It has done this both by enabling disabled people to be active in public life, and by redefining the meaning of disability. But a new question is emerging. Disabled people may have pride and visibility, but do they have power?

(Hasler 1993: 284)

Ken Davis suggests that the movement's very survival was a crucial achievement because:

With this, the tradition of grinning and bearing unjust laws came to an end. The redefinition of disability as a form of social oppression had, in the last resort, validated the public expression of disabled people's deeply felt anger.

(Davis 1993: 290)

CONCLUSIONS: WHAT DOES IT ALL MEAN?

The debate in the previous section has drawn on the views of disabled writers who have combined a political analysis of, with an active involvement in, the movement itself. Few non-disabled analysts or observers have taken the disability movement seriously as a political force, and if they have mentioned it at all, usually it has only been in passing. One recent commentator on disability policy does, however, attempt to address the significance of the rise of the disability movement, albeit from a North Atlantic perspective.

Bickenbach first describes the origins of the movement:

The disablement social movement of the 1970s and 1980s was notable for its focus on self-help and self-empowerment. Although the movement expressed its demands in the language of equality rights, it also pursued various forms of direct political action, such as sit-ins and boycotts, demonstrations, and lobbying activities.

(Bickenbach 1993: 171)

He then goes on to suggest that the tactics of direct action are not simply manoeuvres to achieve particular political or legal goals but also a radical confrontation with, and challenge to, the dominant social order:

What is significant about activism of this sort is that it is intended to be a counter-hegemonic political response to handicapping rather than a legal institutional response. The difference between a demonstration in the streets and a lawsuit may seem to be merely a matter of strategy, but we should not lose sight of the fact that there is a difference between an attempt to destigmatise a group through political empowerment and an attempt to seek specific legal remedies for an individual.

(Bickenbach 1993: 171)

This confrontation with dominant social order, he suggests, represents revolutionary rather than reformist political action:

By its nature, counter-hegemonic politics is far more revolutionary than political agitation directed at specific legislative or political ends. The aim of the former is to attack, directly and dramatically, a dominant societal framework, rather than to use it and the social institutions that make it up in order to win favourable concessions.

(Bickenbach 1993: 171)

It is clear to us that the disability movement in Britain is neither one thing nor the other; in fact it is a movement which incorporates both revolutionary and reformist politics. Our own evaluation of its significance reflects the partisan position we outlined at the beginning of the book; that is that the disability movement is not only important to disabled people. It is increasingly becoming important to everyone because:

The disability movement is moving inexorably to the centre of the stage, and its significance lies not in the legacy it will leave behind, but in the new forms of social relations it will be instrumental in creating.

(Oliver 1990: 93)

In building our own unique movement, we may be not only making our own history but also making a contribution to the history of humankind.

Chapter 10

Interviews with Jane Campbell and Mike Oliver by Bamber Postance

The material in this chapter is based on two separate interviews with Bamber Postance, a postgraduate student at the University of Greenwich and an ally of the disability movement.

BAMBER POSTANCE   In collaboration with other disabled people, you have undertaken what is almost an archaeological expedition examining the foundations of the modern disability movement. I would like to use this interview to allow some of your own personal experiences as active participants in this movement and its campaign for civil and human rights an expression. In addition, I would like to reflect back at you some of the issues raised by disabled participants in your collaborative venture.

Mike Oliver, in this book Judy Hunt has noted how an increase in the self-organisation of disabled people in the 1960s and 1970s, through the development of various groups, was absolutely crucial to the birth of the disability movement. Can I ask you to sketch out your own personal involvement during this period?

MIKE OLIVER   Initially, like many disabled people, I was in a kind of 'denial'. I didn't want to get involved in disability organisations of any kind. But I was active in the paraplegic sports movement, and from that we had to get involved in some political activity because disabled people were in danger of being excluded to make room for the hangers on. So I did get involved in some minor protests. Then, the early 1970s, I went to university and I became interested in left-wing politics more generally. I did know that DIG was around and that people like Paul Hunt and Vic Finkelstein were trying to set up UPIAS, but I suppose, to begin with, I was a self-helper rather than a political analyst. From my own experiences, all of the things I had learnt were due to other disabled people sharing certain experiences with me – how to drive a car, how to get dressed and so forth. I thought that the way to go was to create collective organisations that plugged people in to self-help networks. So, I joined two organisations, SIA and the National Bureau for Handicapped Students – which later became SKILL [National Bureau for Students with Disabilities]. As someone with a spinal injury I thought that SIA offered opportunities which would allow us to live the kind of lives we wanted; and with SKILL, as a disabled student, I thought it was a way to open up higher education to more and more disabled people.

BAMBER POSTANCE   The book shows us the critical importance of UPIAS to the development of the movement, but Ken and Maggie Davis speak of an internal discipline, a weeding out process, within the Union. Can I ask whether you were aware of this aspect of the group, and also about your own involvement with UPIAS?

MIKE OLIVER   On the one hand, with a young family, I didn't feel I had the time to get involved with UPIAS, but also, on the other hand, I have to say that I was suspicious about their discipline and the fact that the collective was all. It was almost as if you couldn't cough or fart without their collective permission – so I always fell shy of that. While I became friends with many people in UPIAS, and I'd known Ken and Maggie before, I never quite got round to joining, and I never joined even in the 1980s.

JANE CAMPBELL   It's important to keep UPIAS in context. Whilst their work was obviously crucial, their membership was only about 200 people at any one time. You can contrast this with BCODP which, having mushroomed in the 1990s, has 106 member organisations representing over 400,000 disabled people.

BAMBER POSTANCE   Mike, can I ask you, at a very general level, how writing this book has influenced your understanding of the rise of the disability movement?

MIKE OLIVER   What the book has made very clear for me is that, first, the rise of the movement in Britain was organised around struggles to get out of residential care with the development of groups such as UPIAS. Second, it was organised around the relative deprivation of disabled people at a time when society was getting richer. This is vitally important to understand. The 1960s was the age of affluence, but the gap between disabled people and the rest of the population widened significantly and disabled people decided that this was no longer acceptable. I think that those are the two most important aspects, if you are talking about cause and effect, and these are the two main reasons why the movement emerged as it did.

BAMBER POSTANCE   Jane, can I ask you now to outline your early involvement in the movement. Micheline Mason has said that, like many other disabled people, she has belonged to the disability movement since childhood. She recalls throwing away the Holy Water from Lourdes, telling Jesus, 'I think they are missing the point.' How far do you personally identify with this?

JANE CAMPBELL   It's strange really, my road to Damascus wasn't as clear as Micheline's and didn't really start until 1983. Before that time I was busily making it in the able-bodied world. I had been in special schools and segregated further education at Hereward College in Coventry, so I had spent a long time with disabled people and I was blaming them for my exclusion from mainstream life. I had never analysed the reasons for my dissatisfaction and I had not formulated any kind of understanding of social oppression. In fact I was very much a disabled person with a condition and taking on the stereotype that disabled people like me were fragile, in need of protection and lots of care – end of story. I blamed the condition for my inability to participate in society rather than looking at any of the real structural and cultural reasons.

So, when I finally made it out into the able-bodied big wide world, I ferociously assimilated all I could, playing totally to other people's agendas. I did the degree and then the masters degree and I really was doing the supercrip trip – proving to everyone that I was as good as – no, better than – any non-disabled person of my age. This was a tough time, both physically and mentally, because I was making considerable sacrifices just to fit in. I had to get over all the barriers of attitude and encounter all the discrimination isolated and alone, and also with arguments that weren't really appropriate.

After completing my education I managed to get a job with a leading disability charity. This was where I finally came out as a disabled person – and not because the organisation liberated or empowered me, quite the opposite! I have to say the experience was not a happy one. But on reflection it was a learning experience, fuelling a passion to change the charitable status quo, and perhaps the story is worth telling because it may have echoes for others who went through similar initiations.

I went into the organisation hoping and thinking that, as a disabled person with all the degrees under the sun, I would be greeted with open arms, and that this would be where I would find supportive and fulfilled employment with opportunities for career development. Unfortunately, the opposite occurred. I remember the first time that I really clocked that however much you tried to be part of the non-disabled world you were never really accepted unless you played a certain role. I was redoing a letter, for the tenth time (they always set me inappropriately physical tasks), and I overheard one of my colleagues speaking on the telephone to a disabled person about transport. She was sweet and informative but when she put the phone down I heard her say to another colleague, 'Oh God, these whingeing disabled people, I hope I don't get another one today because I've got to get on with my work!'. She was not joking, it just was not a joke. I remember thinking, 'This is your work, why are you working here – providing an information service to disabled people – when you actually despise the people you're talking to? Why, why, why?'. And then, my thinking naturally progressed: 'But I'm one of those people', and 'Are they looking at me in the same way?'. It suddenly struck me that maybe there was something more to discrimination than just segregation and access issues. I felt that there was something deeper that I didn't quite understand – but I knew it existed. Within a few months I had left. I wasn't wanted as a colleague but as a token, a window dressing for an organisation that couldn't include me on equal terms.

This was when I first realised that these organisations that were supposedly there to promote and foster disabled people's inclusion in society – it was all a lie. Actually they were there for their own perpetuation, their own self-interest, status and displays of power rather than the promotion and development of disabled people, It was a real pat-on-the-back job – and so I twigged.

BAMBER POSTANCE   Many participants in the movement were significantly influenced by individual disabled people, if you like mentors teaching disability politics. For Richard Wood it was Ken Davis and for Stephen Bradshaw it was Vic Finkelstein. Can I ask about you – if anyone particularly influenced you?

JANE CAMPBELL   After I left the charity I joined the GLC [Greater London Council] – the organisation which allowed a 'thousand flowers to bloom'. And it was there that I got smacked in the face by some very radical disabled people. These people turned me around, they literally got hold of me by the collar and shook me – shook all that internalised oppression out of me. That's when I first learnt about the nature of oppression. They said, 'Look, you feel this way towards other disabled people, stop blaming yourself and other disabled people for the problem. Our problem stems from the barriers in society, prejudicial attitudes and hostile environments.' They gave me the tools to work out the nature of oppression, and once I understood this and how it affected women, black people, older people, lesbians and gays, the whole equal opportunities framework – everything fell into place! I could unpack all the vast amounts of rubbish I had internalised, and it was the most exciting, traumatic yet relieving experience of my life.

I have to name Kirsten Hearn as my first great liberator, and she certainly didn't pull any punches! She was very tough on me. She was involved in SAD, she came from a radical feminist position. She was very uncompromising, but strangely supportive. Kirsten laid it on the line for me and that's what I needed. She was very clear – her arguments were very clear. She retold the story of my life, why I was where I was and why I felt the way I did. When someone can do that for you, in a matter of months, they must be quite special. I have to say I was a complete wreck, suddenly having to rethink everything. And, for a while, I went the other way, denouncing all my poor non-disabled friends and becoming quite a separatist, as I worked through the issues. It's now ten years on, and I still look back on that phase with wonder.

BAMBER POSTANCE   Mike, can I ask the same question of you? Were there any particular individuals who encouraged you to participate in the disability movement and its politics?

MIKE OLIVER   That's a difficult question to answer. I wasn't influenced in the same way as Jane, I suppose because I was part of the initial arguments linking social oppression and disability. Vic [Finkelstein] and I would have arguments around issues, but there was no one disabled person who particularly influenced me in that kind of way. In terms of negative influences, I can think of lots of disabled people I didn't want to be like! If there was one particular influence it was the Fundamental Principles document itself (UPIAS 1976). That was the thing that really spelt it out for me. I am often accused by friends of just recycling the same two ideas in different contexts, of just updating the same two ideas, and if that is the case then those two ideas are in the Fundamental Principles. This seems to me a kind of bible. If it's possible to have a little red book as your hero then the Fundamental Principles is that – it encapsulated all that I thought and all that I still think about disability.

BAMBER POSTANCE   Mike, I am aware that you were involved in some of the development of the BCODP, and particularly in accessing some of the initial funding. Can I ask you to say a little about this?

MIKE OLIVER   Returning to my biography, by the end of the 1970s I had been connected with both the National Bureau and SIA. I left the Bureau in complete disillusionment – basically because they just reproduced all the bad old things about disability charities. The Bureau's management committee was made up of university administrators and lecturers who wanted life to be made easier for themselves;

they were not really committed to opening up higher education to the hordes of disabled people who might come kicking their doors down. I did stay with SIA because they were a dynamic and thrusting organisation. I think SIA is important to the history of the disability movement for two reasons. First, it was the first single-impairment organisation that was run *by* disabled people – it showed the RNIDs [Royal National Institute for the Deaf] and RNIBs that disabled people could do it for themselves. SIA was important in that respect. It was also important in that, from the start of the eighties, SIA was committed to showing that we could develop alternative models of service provision. We built both the SIA welfare service and the national PA scheme in the teeth of opposition from professionals. The Department of Health [DoH] and others said, 'You can't possibly provide welfare services – you're not professionals, you're not trained and you don't have the right sort of accountability networks.' We said, 'Yeah yeah – we'll do it ourselves' – and we did. We demon-strated that disabled people could develop models of service delivery that actually worked. Perhaps the two most important aspects of these services are that disabled people assess themselves and that you are automatically entitled to these services. These were rights. We simply said every SIA member is entitled to X number of days free assistance a year based on their own self-assessment. This revolutionised my life, and the PA scheme was very important to me because it meant I could go to conferences and stay overnight for the first time.

In spite of these successes, by the end of the 1970s, I had progressed enough in my understanding of both the nature of society and the politics around disability issues to know that single-impairment organisations were not enough. It was absolutely clear that single-impairment self-help organ-isations were not going to deliver the goods; they were going to help disabled people in various aspects of their lives, but they weren't actually going to transform disabled people's lives completely. So, along with others, I was concerned to see us develop our own national organisation.

I suppose what really focused it for me was IYDP in 1981. I was very opposed to this, and I went on the radio, the television, wrote articles in the *Guardian* – all over the place – saying what a rotten idea it was. We only seem to have international years for dogs, trees, children or disabled people – never for bank managers or university professors! The whole idea was bound to reinforce notions of dependency and to stigmatise us further, rather than to help us – as its proponents were suggesting.

What became really apparent was that we had no kind of collective voice, nationally, as disabled people; whilst I could express opposition to IYDP, many other people were taking a pragmatic approach. I thought that we ought to have an organisation that could actually debate these things and come up with an authoritative position, not one that I necessarily agreed with. We needed a forum where disabled people could debate whether the international year was a good idea. It was just assumed it was a good thing and then foisted upon us – and of course, as we know now, that is basically what happened!

Consequently, using my position within SIA, I joined Vic Finkelstein and Stephen Bradshaw in promoting the idea of a cross-impairment national organisation, and if we needed such an organisation the sooner we started building it the better! Of course, there was also the whole thing about RI and the birth of DPI. The BCODP's inaugural meeting was held in 1981; I didn't actually go to that and – for the life of me – I cannot remember why! It's interesting reading the accounts of people's recollections; I wasn't there so I don't know what happened. Anyway, once the BCODP was set up I became one of the SIA representatives on its council for four or five years.

I think one of the great untold stories – which doesn't emerge in the book – is just how much the movement owes to SIA. Lots of people talk about how initially there were no resources and how we didn't even have sufficient resources to talk to each other. In one sense this is not true; both Stephen Bradshaw, and Frances Hasler when she joined SIA in 1981, acted as almost unpaid administrators for the BCODP for a considerable period of time – maybe a year or so. SIA was used as a mail drop for the BCODP, quite often the secretarial services and franking machine were used – and, basically, it was all done on the quiet! Stephen and

Frances and myself, as a member of the management committee, knew about it, and when the opportunity came up at SIA committee meetings I always said what a wonderful idea the BCODP was and that we should support it – we always got a general endorsement. But I think had the committee been aware of the extent of support SIA was actually providing for the BCODP they would not have been happy! I do think that this support was at a crucial time for the BCODP, and it ought to be recorded. The BCODP would have never got off the ground in the way it did without SIA.

The second important point was that SIA had developed quite a good relationship with officials at the DoH. Stephen and I among others had managed to extract quite a few Section 64 grants and we used to go to the Department regularly, perhaps every two years, to renew the grants. Clearly, once the BCODP was established the question quickly came up of whether we could get any government funding, so we made an application for a Section 64 grant as a new organisation. Duly we were summoned to the Elephant and Castle – it was myself, Anne Rae and Francine White who went representing the BCODP.

From the outset of the meeting it was immediately clear that the officials were very suspicious of the BCODP. I think that had a lot to do with the overt and covert attacks on us by the disability establishment; we were caricatured as a bunch of loony left-wing Marxists! Selwyn Goldsmith, when he won the Harding man of the year award, devoted some of his speech to the theme! It was probably true that Vic and I were Marxist – I still am although I don't know whether Vic is – but as for the rest of them! I mean, the idea that Stephen Bradshaw is a Marxist is just absurd! But these people used their positions to rubbish the BCODP as some kind of insignificant left-wing organisation, and this did make things difficult. The officials at the Department were already struggling with the idea of disabled people being in charge of their own organisation! Luckily SIA had established a credible relationship with the Department, we had been returning to the Elephant and Castle for a number of years and we had proved to be responsible, and I think it was partly this established credibility that enabled us to get that first Section 64 grant – £10,000 per year for three years I think it was – despite all the rubbishing and denigrating of the BCODP that had gone on behind the scenes.

I remember the actual meeting very well. The Thatcher government had cut back Section 64 grants and the officials kept saying to us, 'It's all very well coming here but we have to cut our funds anyway – where are we going to get the money from to fund you as a new organisation?'. My initial tack was, 'That's what you get paid for, you get paid to make those decisions – not us. Give us a consultancy and we will tell you where to get it!'. But, clearly, that would not cut any ice. So we said, 'Well, you have got to look at the way the money is allocated. How many Section 64 grants are given to democratic and accountable organisations?'. But, again, that was not enough and they kept pushing. So, finally I said, 'How much are you giving to RADAR? What does RADAR do? If you really want to know how to fund the BCODP, take the money from RADAR!'. But, of course, they never did and they still haven't to this day.

BAMBER POSTANCE   Jane, can I follow this issue of resources a little further. Your work has shown that the movement and the BCODP have never been driven by a motivation to become rich and self-perpetuating. Having said that, effective resourcing is obviously an issue. Would you like to say anything on these issues?

JANE CAMPBELL   I can tell you what I definitely don't want to see: I don't want us to go down the road of having such a well-oiled, well-resourced infrastructure that all the main activists become slick professionals, caught up in expensive and elitist bureaucracies. The BCODP should never be a second-tier service provider to the current services that exist for disabled people. I don't want to see us go down that route because it will threaten our campaigning role. In a way (and I'm probably going to get lynched for saying this), the fact that we have been so badly resourced has – to a point – been a strength and to our advantage. People have put their power and energies into the BCODP on a voluntary basis with no financial carrots. The BCODP activists have been so motivated by their anger, frustration and desire for change that they have participated in a highly principled and genuine way. This has undoubtedly strengthened our struggle.

We have never been about accessing resources simply to expand the organisation's office. Any money we do obtain goes straight to campaigning projects or strengthening our membership of disabled people and their interest groups. This involvement of grassroots disabled people has given us our principled approach, our non-compromising stance, and it is the organisation's hallmark that has kept us basically on line. We have never compromised to the extent of traditional disability charities. Others may say, for example, 'OK, we can have segregation here or we can tolerate piece-meal civil rights legislation there.' We have always said that disabled people will not be free citizens until we have full control of our own lives. We haven't been bought off and we have got a vision. At the present time, if we were given sufficient resources we would undoubtedly 'fly'. We need resources to feed our campaigns and to strengthen our vast membership. Now we have crystallised our position, our aims and our objectives, we have an understanding of disability as a civil and human rights issue.

Where a lack of resources really has restricted the BCODP is we have never had enough money to involve and develop disabled people and their organisations to their full potential. We don't want money to professionalise the BCODP's infrastructure or to provide a bigger building, more staff or managers. Where we have lost out is having resources to enable people with learning difficulties, the small black disabled persons' group or the mental health systems survivors' group, to participate in the BCODP seminars, conferences, events and debates that are going on.

BAMBER POSTANCE   So you need long-term revenue funding to have a dialogue with your own constituency?

JANE CAMPBELL   Yes, yes, but not just a dialogue, although that is part – to allow all our membership organisations to fully participate in the disability movement. That's exactly what has held us back.

BAMBER POSTANCE   Jane, within the book forcible arguments have been made against the non-compromising tactics used by the BCODP and the disability movement against the traditional disability establishment in the 1980s. In particular, the movement's tactics have been criticised as being unnecessarily conflictual. Should the BCODP have been more co-operative? Second, there is the argument that the BCODP has had an unhelpful and continuing focus on rights instead of service provision. With a view to the future, can I ask you to comment on these two criticisms?

JANE CAMPBELL   In the mid-eighties the BCODP was still in a process of maturing, and so I would say that, at times, we were probably too confrontational and we might have lost some support, but at other times we were not confrontational enough. The absence of visible direct action in the streets was to our detriment, because it is only since we have taken to the streets that we have been visible in the media. Our Elephant and Castle 'Rights Not Charity' demonstration was perhaps the watershed in terms of public/political relations. Hundreds of disabled people, demanding a platform, managed to break all the stereotypes and get through to the general public. Thus, I do think that being confrontational, though I prefer to call it challenging, has been a necessary part of our maturing process.

Every group goes through an angry phase; every person when they become liberated and come to recognise the injustices they have been tolerating for years gets very, very angry. In fact, I think we were brilliant not to have been more confrontational, we have been amazingly restrained! I certainly felt exceedingly confrontational – and rightly so in the face of quite aggressive discrimination from, most notably, the charity sector. To say that it was a mistake to express that anger and frustration is both naive and wrong. Expressing anger gives disabled people a certain confidence and a strength; the point is to capture and direct that fury into a positive direction.

This was – and remains – the job of the BCODP. Yes, members were angry and we had a right to be angry and anger is necessary. Some sections of the community may get very frightened, touchy and freaked out about disabled people becoming angry, perhaps because we are emerging from our passive, safe stereotypes and becoming powerful human beings.

BAMBER POSTANCE   Mike, can I ask you for your viewpoint

on these two criticisms of the BCODP's relationship with traditional disability organisations?

MIKE OLIVER   I also believe the critique is wrong, in terms of both the political analysis and its criticism of the movement. In terms of the politics, we had to do it that way. We had to do it for ourselves. In the 1960s and 1970s many of us had direct experience of being involved with the big charity battalions. There was no way that they could be taken over or subverted or made democratically accountable – and history will judge their records. If you look at all the key issues that we now talk about, whether it is in service provision, rights or whatever; all of these have arisen from our attempts to collectively self-organise and absolutely none have emerged from the big battalions.

As one example, when we said we wanted ADL most of the charities said, 'No thank you, our members don't want that – it's being too confrontational and too conflictual.' My perception is that these organisations did not change because there were moles working from the inside, they changed because we became so powerful externally that they had no choice. They didn't want to look like what they are – which is nineteenth-century remnants with no place in a modern welfare state.

I also think it is wrong to criticise the BCODP in terms of its service provision record. As Jane has said, the BCODP has never had the resources! I refuse to believe that if the BCODP had the resources, of let us say the Spastics Society or MENCAP, that they wouldn't do a far better job. If you look at what the BCODP is beginning to provide, through its IL Committee and its promotion of PA schemes all over the country; all of this is coming from the organisations of disabled people themselves and not from the old charities. The ironic thing is the faster they run to catch up, the more they produce these trendy small group homes and supposed IL schemes, the more they cock it up. They still couldn't organise a piss-up in a brewery!

One of the things I've written about quite extensively is that organisations like these, the Royal National Institutes, SCOPE and RADAR, are not just irrelevant to the lives of disabled people: they are actually downright dangerous.

Why are they dangerous? For two reasons, one because they give the impression that society cares and is doing something useful, but second because they take money and resources away from the BCODP and organisations controlled by disabled people. Therefore they are not an irrelevance and I see a time, at some point in the future, when they may become the target of political action. At the end of the day, and as the movement gets bigger and more powerful and as it needs more and more resources, we may actually have to target some of those organisations. The kinds of critiques we have applied to state welfare may have to be applied to the state charities – which is what these organisations are – state charity. Again, returning to the Fundamental Principles document, there was a whole section about state charity, but we have never got around to undertaking the theoretical and practical work on this issue. That doesn't mean to say that we won't get around to doing it over the next few years.

BAMBER POSTANCE   Jane, following the enactment of comprehensive ADL for disabled people, how would you like to see the relationship between organisations controlled by disabled people and the traditional disability establishment proceed, or would you like to see a split?

JANE CAMPBELL   The only reason that disabled people have gained power and status in this country has been by coming together in our own organisations and going through the process of liberation. I hope that this won't stop and that BCODP and its constituent organisations will be at the heart of this process.

Personally, with regard to traditional organisations, it's a difficult question. I think the jury is out on this one at the moment. At this moment in our history I believe it's impossible to turn around an organisation that has existed for eighty or ninety years, that is highly paternalistic, that bases its whole approach around research, cure and the eradication of the problem which they see to be as disabled people's impairments. Because of the sheer energy needed to turn round these super-tanker charities we might as well start with a clean sheet of paper.

The help that these organisations have given to disabled

people has been infinitesimal when compared with the hindrance that they have caused and damage they have inflicted. They have influenced disabled people to reject their bodies and minds, to regard their impairments as a tragedy which must be eradicated at any price, and to return to some mythical perception of undamaged normality. They have inflicted vast damage to disabled people's self worth. So, I would say that I would like to see an end to the impairment charities.

However, I do see a role for non-disabled people and other interest groups as allies in our organisations and our movement. The BCODP has recently made a highly successful alliance with Liberty, working together on human rights, and we have just produced a report called 'Access Denied'. So I wouldn't like to say that people committed to disability issues working within these traditional organisations shouldn't be part of organisations that are run and controlled by disabled people. The BCODP has fostered very good working relations with professionals working at, say, RNIB and RADAR, but when we work with them it has to be on our terms and to our own agenda.

BAMBER POSTANCE   Jane, ignoring for a moment the essential conflicts between the traditional disability establishment and the disability movement, your book has also made it clear that there are tensions within the movement itself. Can I ask how writing this book has contributed to your understanding of these tensions?

JANE CAMPBELL   Obviously, there are huge tensions between various interest groups in the BCODP, but as long as we grapple with our differences in-house and don't put our dirty washing out to the world, that's fine. There are far too many bodies waiting to divide us and rule the disability movement. Differences are very important and conflicts have been creative for the movement. Perhaps what emerges most strongly from the book is how important it is to respect where people come from, their experiences and why they may have come to their various viewpoints. The book has taught me that liberation can take many forms and that there are many interpretations of one single event. Who knows who is right? Of course no single person is, they all have a point of view. The aim of the movement and the BCODP must be to take in all these differences, this jigsaw of opinion, and to work towards a common consensus, a democratic way forward. We must listen to other people more about the direction they see for the BCODP. The deaf community may not be right, People First may not be right – but between us there is a way forward, a strength in unity within the BCODP.

When you first become emancipated and liberated you grab on to very focused principles – principles that you will not deviate from; but you have to learn to value different ideas and interpretations. I have also learnt to listen to what non-disabled people have to say and think about our movement and to address their views. I used to rubbish people sometimes simply because of their label, 'social worker', 'doctor', 'non-disabled', or whatever, before I had heard what they had to say. I was stereotyping them as I had been stereotyped.

BAMBER POSTANCE   Perhaps a valid mistake!

JANE CAMPBELL   Yes! But, I would also do it with disabled people. I would see someone, for example from SIA, and think, 'Oh God – here comes a middle-class, white, supercrip wheelchair user who just wants to be normal!'. To an extent I was right – people with spinal injuries do have a certain experience and of course this will inform their view of the world and themselves. This experience and its articulation is no less valid than mine. What this book has taught me is to analyse our various experiences of oppression and to work with those in finding an inclusive and an embracing way forward for the movement.

BAMBER POSTANCE   Ann MacFarlane particularly, but also Nasa Begum and Micheline Mason, have expressed fears about the somewhat dogmatic approach of the disability movement. Whilst your book has made it abundantly clear that understanding disability as a form of social oppression lies at the very heart of the movement, it is also apparent that many disabled people, especially those disabled people not yet involved in the movement, find this understanding difficult, perhaps especially with regards to the distinction between illness and disability. How would you respond?

JANE CAMPBELL   Instead of rubbishing these worries in any way, instead of saying that we will not deviate from our understandings or dilute our stance, we have to say, 'Let's have a look, again, at these issues. Let's have a dialogue.' Having said that, disabled people must learn to differentiate between illness, impairment and disability. In doing so we will teach the non-disabled community the real meaning of the social model. To me, the social model embraces disabled people who are ill, and disabled people who are ill must be treated in the same way as able-bodied people who are sick: with appropriate care, sympathy and understanding. We want parity of treatment – but not an oppressive medicalisation of our lives.

BAMBER POSTANCE   Mike, Phillip Mason and Ann MacFarlane have recognised how essential it is for the movement to continue educating the mass of disabled people about disability; Sian Vasey has noted how a new career path has opened up for some disabled people to undertake this vital task. Can I ask for your views on this issue?

MIKE OLIVER   Clearly one of the major issues that the movement has to confront is the recognition that, for the vast majority of disabled people, having an impairment is still an individualising experience. The question is how the movement can address the collectivising of individual experience, whether in a day centre, special schools, residential home or in the community. It's how you confront that issue, how you speak to people wherever they are, whatever their circumstances, and make them feel the things you are saying are relevant to them – it's how you create an accessible movement so that people can join in that is crucial. Jane has outlined some of the developments in the BCODP and, as your question implies, disability equality training has been important. I have to say that I think the disability movement has done magnificently in less than fifteen years – it's now remarkable how many disabled people, although perhaps still a minority, do actually feel part of a collective movement.

JANE CAMPBELL   We do need to continue building a dialogue with every member. But we mustn't forget our successes, for example through the PA newsletter, through the empowerment courses disabled people have organised, through the media and local organisations, through the IL movement and its policy initiatives, and also through our civil rights campaign.

BAMBER POSTANCE   Jane, with reference to this, can I ask you a very specific question. Vic Finkelstein has argued that a critical task for the movement is to develop a national policy on disability: a vision for the future. He suggests that the process by which such a vision is generated is of vital importance, and that disabled people throughout Britain should be collectively drawn into creating such a vision. Can I ask for your views on this proposal?

JANE CAMPBELL   The BCODP is in the process, and has been over the last two years, of working with organisations of disabled people and disabled individuals up and down the country to produce a policy in all the twelve key areas of discrimination – like education, employment, politics. We are about to present our policy on IL and direct payments, which was the result of a national conference with all the leaders in the IL movement – a big think-tank. This is only our latest policy development; it all really started after Colin Barnes' book [Barnes 1991].

As to the second part of your question, the process by which we involve people in the BCODP; I remember in 1985 when I was taken along to my first BCODP conference and AGM [annual general meeting], I witnessed great long speeches by Ken Davis, Vic Finkelstein and Anne Rae – and I thought,'Oh my God, how am I ever going to be able to absorb and then articulate stuff like that?'. A lot of it was way above my head, and if I had a criticism of the disability movement at that time it was because it was so intellectually inaccessible. You really did need quite a trained analytical mind to participate. The BCODP was run by highly intelligent academic disabled people who were more interested in the philosophies and principles rather than how to get new disabled people on board and practical outcomes. I came away from that conference feeling very excited, very intellectually challenged but also very frustrated, because I knew it was going to take a hell of a long time to get tangible results. In the beginning I didn't have a hope in hell of competing with these 'big brains', I felt disempowered. I resolved then that if I ever did become involved and active within the BCODP I would bloody well make sure that its brilliant ideas, its brilliant notions and brilliant philosophy – its sheer excitement – were going to be accessible to other disabled people. In my four years as Chair of the BCODP we have attempted to democratise the structures of the BCODP, opening it up to individual memberships and sharing responsibilities. We've created a structure so that different groups of disabled people can move in and out, with more support for sub-groups, conferences and seminars. This is perhaps what Vic meant by the importance of the process. We want people to know about these wonderful ideas – of the social model and liberation. We also want them to use them!

Today it is possible to be involved in the disability movement in a number of ways: through the arts, through the IL movement, through direct action and the campaign for civil rights, through membership of the BCODP and local organisations and coalitions of disabled people. The movement is a jigsaw – each piece is vital for the true picture to emerge.

BAMBER POSTANCE   In respect of the movement's campaign for comprehensive ADL: it seems to me that there is a false premise in some of the discussions around this at present – that somehow it is just around the corner. What are your views?

JANE CAMPBELL   I am afraid that I am less optimistic than some people. I think that the optimism has come from being involved in the Rights Now campaign, and sometimes you have to believe that what you are fighting for is just around the corner. But also I think that we have been scuppered by a very clever government that has dressed up a cake to look like ADL, but unfortunately the ingredients are all rotten and the cake will taste disgusting to disabled people.

This deviousness has made it appear to some MPs and the general public that we do not need to rethink and redraft new ADL for disabled people – but we do! The current Conservative proposals will never gain disabled people civil rights – there is discrimination within the bill itself! However, when the bill is passed we will have to show the public the differences between this statute and true civil rights legislation. This is a very difficult message to communicate, but if we fail we are lost. What is particularly depressing is broken commitments. The Labour Party, who have always been with us and had committed themselves to bringing in civil rights legislation in their first term, are beginning to renege on their promise. They are now saying that maybe we just need a commission in addition to the Conservative bill. Why do we need a commission to enforce the unenforceable?

When I started dabbling in politics, with the civil rights bill, I was very naive. I felt that our arguments were so clear and right, so based on principles of rights and justice, that finally politicians would grasp the nettle. How naive I was! We have to understand what makes them tick, and whilst I don't think that we should make deals, we have to understand what we are up against. We have to be political too – in some respects. It's not a clean game and it's a horrible area to be involved in! But that is how our political structure works, and if you don't play, don't get in there and operate to your advantage, you're lost. That was a problem with the BCODP in the early 1980s; it was too highly principled, politically correct and separatist to actually make things happen.

So, as to your question: I don't think we'll see it in the next few years. The government bill offers enough to keep the punters happy and has considerably diluted our campaign. We shall have to demonstrate, all over again, the discrimination that disabled people experience daily. It is quite depressing. I see proper ADL as being a number of years away... but it will happen.

BAMBER POSTANCE   Mike, have you anything to add to these views?

MIKE OLIVER   I can see ADL being passed, once the political parties get the message that it's in their political interest to do so. That's not the problem. The problem is that they know they're not going to have to enforce it! So, I would want to broaden the question out. I have always been clear that legislation by itself is not the answer, whether it's ADL, legislation for PA – whatever. Frankly, I'm as suspicious of legal rights as Marx was a hundred years ago when he called them a 'bourgeois notion'.

BAMBER POSTANCE   A cover story, a formal equality without
    any content?

MIKE OLIVER   As I've said in my previous book on *The Politics
    of Disablement*, we need three things in combination: state-
    guaranteed rights, plus proper funding for organisations
    controlled and run by disabled people themselves, plus
    freedom of information. We do need to be able to access all
    the details within the agencies paid to control us and keep us
    down. Most disabled people are not going to have access to
    the resources they need to enforce their statutory rights, and
    this is why I am arguing that we need a strong, vibrant
    disability movement to take that on board. We should not let
    people off the hook nor let the courts be sole arbiter of what is
    right and just.

BAMBER POSTANCE   Can I ask you a broad question now:
    perhaps we could discuss the links between media percep-
    tions of the disability movement and general representations
    of disabled people, which, perhaps overwhelmingly, are
    underpinned by a portrayal of disabled people as economic
    and social burdens?

JANE CAMPBELL   Whilst the public are beginning to acknowl-
    edge that disabled people should have rights of access to
    buildings, a right to get in a cinema or a restaurant, they still
    can't quite make that intellectual leap of understanding what
    really empowered disabled people could do in terms of
    becoming productive and contributing members of society.
    Society has to develop its understanding of inclusion even
    further. People do not understand, for instance, the issue
    around PA for disabled people and direct payments. They
    haven't seen severely impaired disabled people actually turn
    their lives around. Let's take a very simple and personal
    example. When I show people the way I live, how I organise
    my home and how productive I am, they're absolutely gob-
    smacked. And these are people, remember, who know of me,
    know of my work and understand disability as a rights issue.
    Yet, at the end of the day, they are still grappling to really
    understand. They cannot conceptualise the true inclusion of
    disabled people, as empowered citizens within society. They

still think, 'Jane's great, but at the end of the day she's still a burden because she has to be looked after.' They don't recognise that personal autonomy is about controlling one's life and that personal independence can be facilitated through another body.

If people could really perceive the personal growth of disabled people when they become PA users, when they are given full control over their own lives, they would begin to understand the nature of oppression against disabled people. They would become committed to challenging this oppression. We haven't got far enough in understanding what full civil rights, human rights, for disabled people could do to break down and demolish this idea of burden.

So, on the one hand you have people who may understand the idea of rights but, on the other, they still see the rising cost of care, because of the ageing population, and the media still focuses on people getting up, going to bed, the basic looking after. Disabled people and older people are infantilised in this debate. When people think of looking after someone they think of looking after their kids, so people only have one view of what care means.

That's the kind of uncomfortable and massive contradiction people cannot quite get over in their heads. It's the complexities of what it means to be an interdependent person, because we are all interdependent – none of us are independent. We all rely on others and support structures for our lives; the issue is whether disabled people have self-determination within the structures that support us or whether we have structures that make us dependent.

BAMBER POSTANCE   So, you would understand the IL movement as an essential resource in the development of the movement?

JANE CAMPBELL   It is going to be the IL movement that probably brings disabled people together. Why? Because under the responsibilities of cash for care, people have to come together for support, information and advice. And that's certainly been shown in many areas where the local IL schemes are more proactive with more participants than the majority of local associations and coalitions of disabled people.

BAMBER POSTANCE   Do you regard PA to be the key for unlocking civil rights?

JANE CAMPBELL   It's going to be one of the keys. IL does free up disabled people to expend their energies in other ways, which may be campaigns for civil rights, for inclusive education, accessible transport, or campaigns against discriminatory LA charging policies. PA has freed me up to spend enormous energies on political issues. If I hadn't had PA I would never have been such an effective Chair of the BCODP – there's no doubt about that. Many of the key activists within the BCODP are PA users: is this a coincidence?

BAMBER POSTANCE   I am aware that in the book People First have criticised the movement not for exclusion, but rather for a failure to actively include people with learning difficulties. I know there have been developments in this respect: would you like to say something about this – perhaps linking it to the themes of IL and PA?

JANE CAMPBELL   Again, I see it as the next development. At the beginning of the BCODP the big thinkers needed to come together and think through some of the principles and to lay foundations. And then we, the mass of disabled people, wandered in and took the organisations down other, very dynamic paths. I think People First are currently taking the BCODP down a very dynamic path. They will open it up and make it more accessible to a whole host of new disabled people, not just people with a learning difficulty. Through their very open and blunt criticisms of the ways in which we can be exclusive, about the way we run our organisation and the ways we can be quite cliquey, People First are challenging us to continue to open up. We started very exclusively and perhaps we needed to be exclusive at that time. Some people find this opening up very hard, but this is the process of inclusion; it's the process of becoming a mass democratic movement of all disabled people, and not just a bunch of white wheelchair users!

BAMBER POSTANCE   Would you see the movement taking its ideas of IL and PA into the new institutionalisation of group homes?

JANE CAMPBELL   It's something I want to see explored and discussed with people with learning difficulties. But we have to recognise how difficult it is for disabled people going into institutions to promote IL, both practically and emotionally. For disabled people who have experienced institutionalisation, and for those who fear it, such a process is painful and difficult. As individuals, we have to be both empowered and liberated to be able to manage this effectively. But this process is a vital one and there are already a number of people with learning difficulties, up and down the country, who are directly controlling their own lives with direct payments. And why not?

BAMBER POSTANCE   Mike, what do you see as being the distinguishing characteristics of the British disability movement's IL philosophy?

MIKE OLIVER   From the early 1980s, Ken Davis and the DCDP recognised that there has always been a distinction between what we mean by IL in Britain and what they meant in the States. IL in America is organised around self-empowerment, individual rights and the idea that in the land of the free and the home of the brave – all that crap – individuals, if they are given access under the law and the constitution, can be independent. In contrast, in Britain – and Ken in Derbyshire has always been clear about this – IL entailed collective responsibilities for each other and a collective organisation. IL wasn't about individual self-empowerment; it was about individuals helping one another. Once you accept that notion, it seems to me, you are beginning to question the foundations of the society in which we live. It is bizarre for people to think that we, as disabled people, can live in Britain with full civil rights and all the services we need without fundamental changes. We are not actually talking about tinkering around at the edges of society to let people in. For disabled people to play a full part in British society, this society will have to change fundamentally. The bottom line is that people with impairments are always going to be disadvantaged in hierarchical societies – I cannot see anywhere in history where that hasn't been the case. I don't think many people in the movement recognise that – it is not just a case of ADL tomorrow.

BAMBER POSTANCE   This is something that you, Colin Barnes and Jenny Morris have been hinting at in the literature for a while – normally on the last lines of articles and chapters! Perhaps these perceptions have not been stated clearly enough. Is this what you understand by a vision for the future of the disability movement, and if so how do you see a realisation of the vision?

MIKE OLIVER   The answer to the last question is that politicising people with impairments around disability issues is one stage in our development. We must go on and politicise ourselves around other issues – other oppressions if you like – and ultimately politicise ourselves around the very nature of a society which oppresses a whole range of different groups. To stop at understanding oppression solely on the grounds of impairment seems to me to inevitably end in a position where disabled people will continue to be oppressed and discriminated against. There does need to be a much broader vision at the end of it, because for disabled people to be truly free we have to live in a truly free society.

Glossary

Asian People with Disabilities Alliance   One of the first organisations representing people from ethnic minorities to become part of the disability movement.

Berkeley CIL   The first centre for independent living, which pioneered the modern philosophy of self-determination rather than living independently.

Blind Register   A national register of blind people eligible for a particular state benefit.

Cheshire Foundation   A charity, established by Group Captain Leonard Cheshire after World War II, which set out to provide residential homes to severely disabled people.

Creasey, Richard   A former ITV current affairs documentary and features producer/executive. Co-founder of *LINK*.

Electric cars   One of the first specialised vehicles authorised to travel on public highways and supplied to disabled people free of charge from the Department of Social Security.

Enns, Henry   The first salaried director of Disabled People's International.

GEMMA   An organisation for disabled lesbians and gay men and their partners.

Goldsmith, Selwyn   The author of *Designing for the Disabled*, the first comprehensive encyclopedia of how to design accessible environments for disabled people.

Grove Road   A specialised housing scheme for disabled people.

Hereward College   One of the first segregated further education colleges offering a range of academic qualifications to disabled people for whom traditional educational routes were perceived to be inaccessible or inappropriate.

Independence 92 Vancouver   A conference dedicated to themes on independent living around the world. Over a thousand disabled delegates attended, representing over ninety countries.

Ingram, Pat   The producer of *LINK* after Richard Creasey.

Integration Alliance   An organisation campaigning for the end of segregated education and the introduction of inclusive education for all children regardless of impairment.

Joint Committee on Mobility   A committee of organisations and individuals representing disabled people's transport interests. Its particular remit was the introduction and development of Motability and the Mobility Allowance.

Leaman, Dick   One of the founder members of the Union of the Physically Impaired Against Segregation and the first Disabled People's International UK Representative.

Le Court   A Leonard Cheshire Residential Home in Hampshire famous for the radical direct action of its residents.

Liberty   A UK organisation campaigning for human and civil rights for all sections of the community.

LINK   The longest-running continuous magazine programme for disabled people, in production for twenty years.

Living Options   A project set up by the King's Fund Centre to develop and promote a greater range of community living support services for disabled people.

Massey, Bert   The first disabled director of RADAR.

MENCAP   The largest organisation working for people with learning difficulties and their families in Britain.

MIND   A national organisation for people experiencing mental health difficulties.

Muscle Power   An organisation of people with a neuromuscular impairment.

Noddy car   A colloquial term for the standard Department of Social Security electric car or three-wheeled vehicle.

Papworth   A UK hospital and rehabilitation centre.

People First   A national organisation of people with learning difficulties.

Powerhouse   A refuge and community centre for women with learning difficulties.

REGARD   The national representative organisation of disabled lesbians and gays.

Rehabilitation International   An international organisation concerned with rehabilitation and run largely by doctors and other professionals.

Rights Now   A national coalition of organisations for and of disabled people campaigning for fully comprehensive anti-discrimination legislation.

Roberts, Ed   The co-founder of the first centre for independent living, and co-founder and director of the World Institute on Disability.

SCOPE   An organisation for people with cerebral palsy and their families, which has recently changed its name from the Spastics Society.

SKILL   National Bureau for Students with Disabilities

Social model   A definition and analysis of disability initiated by the Union of the Physically Impaired Against Segregation in the 1970s and later developed by Vic Finkelstein and Mike Oliver; a crucial philosophy that underpins and informs the direction of the disability movement.

Spastics Society   *See* SCOPE.

Townsend, Peter   One of the founders of the Disability Alliance, known for his income approach to disability issues, and an academic who has published extensively on poverty.

Treloars   The only grammar school for disabled people with mixed impairments.

White, Francine   A key activist in the early days of the British Council of Disabled People and Disabled People's International.

World Congress   A four-yearly gathering of the World Council of Disabled People's International (DPI) and DPI members to elect officers and vote on policy change.

Bibliography

Abberley P (1987) 'The Concept of Oppression and the Development of a Social Theory of Disability' *Disability, Handicap and Society* Vol 2 No 1.

Altman D (1994) *Power and Community: Organizational and Community Responses to AIDS* London: Taylor and Francis.

Atkinson D and Shakespeare P (1993) 'Introduction' in Shakespeare P, Atkinson D and French S (eds) *Reflecting on Research Practice* Buckingham: Open University Press.

Barnes C (1991) *Disabled People in Britain and Discrimination* London: Hurst & Co.

Barnes C and Oliver M (1995) 'Disability Rights: Rhetoric and Reality in the UK' *Disability and Society* Vol 10 No 1.

Begum N, Hill M and Stevens S (1994) (eds) *Reflections: Views of Black Disabled People on their Lives and Community Care* London: Central Council for Education and Training in Social Work.

Benford R and Hunt A (1995) 'Dramaturgy and Social Movements: The Social Construction and Communication of Power' in Lyman (1995a).

Bickenbach J (1993) *Physical Disability and Social Policy* Toronto: University of Toronto Press.

Blumer H (1995) 'Social Movements' in Lyman (1995a).

Bottomore T and Rubel M (1963) (eds) *Karl Marx: Selected Writings in Sociology and Social Philosophy* Harmondsworth: Penguin.

Calhoun C (1994) (ed.) *Social Theory and the Politics of Identity* Oxford: Blackwell.

Campling J (1981) (ed.) *Images of Ourselves* London: Routledge & Kegan Paul.

CORAD (1982) 'Report by the Committee on Restrictions Against Disabled People' London: HMSO.

Dalton R and Kuechler M (1990) (eds) *Challenging the Political Order: New Social and Political Movements in Western Democracies* Cambridge: Polity Press.

Davis K (1993) 'On the Movement' in Swain *et al.* (1993).

Davis K and Mullender A (1993) *Ten Turbulent Years* Nottingham: Centre for Social Action, University of Nottingham.

Despouy L (1993) *Human Rights and Disability* New York: United Nations Economic and Social Council.

De Swaan A (1990) *The Management of Normality: Critical Essays in Health and Welfare* London: Routledge.

Driedger D (1989) *The Last Civil Rights Movement* London: Hurst and Co.

Freeden M (1991) *Rights* Milton Keynes: Open University Press.

French S (1994) (ed.) *On Equal Terms: Working with Disabled People* Oxford: Butterworth-Heinemann.

Friedman J (1992) *Empowerment: The Politics of Alternative Development* Oxford: Blackwell.

Gillespie-Sells K and Ruebain D (1992) 'Double the Trouble, Twice the Fun'. London: Channel 4 Television Publications.

Hasler F (1993) 'Developments in the Disabled People's Movement' in Swain *et al.* (1993).

Hevey D (1992) *The Creatures Time Forgot: Photography and Disability Imagery* London: Routledge.

Humphreys S and Gordon P (1992) *Out of Sight: The Experience of Disability 1900–1950* Plymouth: Northcote House Publishers.

Hunt P (1966) (ed.) *Stigma* London: Geoffrey Chapman.

Inglehart R (1990) 'Values, Ideology and Cognitive Mobilization in New Social Movements' in Dalton and Kuechler (1990).

Jones S (1994) '"Civil Rights" and the Normalisation of Class-Rule' *Coalition* November.

Kemmis S and McTaggart R (1988) (eds) *The Action Research Planner* Victoria: Deakin University Press.

Lyman S (1995a) (ed.) *Social Movements: Critiques, Concepts, Case-Studies* Basingstoke: Macmillan.

Lyman S (1995b) 'Social Theory and Social Movements: Sociology as Sociodicy' in Lyman (1995a).

Marx G and McAdam D (1994) *Collective Behaviour and Social Movements* Englewood Cliffs, NJ: Prentice Hall.

Morris J (1991) *Pride Against Prejudice* London: Women's Press.

Morris J (1992) 'Personal and Political: A Feminist Perspective in Researching Physical Disability' *Disability, Handicap and Society* Vol 7 No 2.

Morris J (1996) *Feminism and Disability* London: Women's Press.

Morrow R (1994) *Critical Theory and Methodology* London: Sage.

Oliver M (1984) 'The Politics of Disability' *Critical Social Policy* Vol 11.

Oliver M (1990) *The Politics of Disablement* Basingstoke: Macmillan.

Oliver M (1992) 'Changing the Social Relations of Research Production' *Disability, Handicap and Society* Vol 7 No 2.

Oliver M (1995) *Understanding Disability: From Theory To Practice* Basingstoke: Macmillan.

Oliver M and Barnes C (1995) 'Disability Rights: Rhetoric and Reality in the UK' *Disability and Society* Vol 10 No 1.

Oliver M and Hasler F (1987) 'Disability and Self Help: A Case Study of the Spinal Injuries Association' *Disability, Handicap and Society* Vol 2 No 2.

Oliver M and Zarb G (1989) 'The Politics of Disability: A New Approach' *Disability, Handicap and Society* Vol 4 No 3.

Pagel M (1988) *On Our Own Behalf: An Introduction to the Self-Organisation of Disabled People* Manchester: GMCDP Publications.

Scotch R (1984) *From Goodwill to Civil Rights: Transforming Federal Disability Policy* Philadelphia: Temple University Press.

Scott A (1990) *Ideology and New Social Movements* London: Unwin Hyman.

Shakespeare T (1993) 'Disabled People's Self-Organisation: A New Social Movement?' *Disability, Handicap and Society* Vol 8 No 3.

Stuart O (1992) 'Race and Disability: What Type of Double Disadvantage?' *Disability, Handicap and Society* Vol 7 No 2.

Swain J, Finkelstein V, French S and Oliver M (1993) *Disabling Barriers – Enabling Environments* London: Sage.

Topliss E (1979) *Provision for the Disabled* Oxford: Blackwell.

Touraine A (1981) *The Voice and the Eye: An Analysis of Social Movements* Cambridge: Cambridge University Press.

Touraine A (1995) 'Beyond Social Movements' in Lyman (1995a).

UPIAS (1976) 'Fundamental Principles of Disability' (a summary document of the discussion held on 22 November 1975 between UPIAS and DA) London: UPIAS.

Wood P (1980) *International Classification of Impairments, Disabilities and Handicaps* Geneva: World Health Organisation.

Woodwill G (1993) *Independent Living and Participation in Research* Toronto: Centre for Independent Living in Toronto (CILT).

Zarb G and Oliver M (1993) *Ageing with a Disability: What Do they Expect after All These Years?* London: University of Greenwich.

Index